## Praise for *From the Edge of the World*:

"A great book! After reading it, I relived times spent in the countries I had visited, and I felt like I had been to those which I had not. [Roger Blackwell] not only teaches us important lessons about business, but also about life."
  —Jack Kahl, chief executive officer and chairman, MANCO, INC.

"[Blackwell] has always been a no-nonsense professor and businessman who tells it like it is . . . and this is his format for a no-nonsense look at how the world really works."
  —Dave Thomas, founder, Wendy's International

"Competing on a global basis requires a keen understanding of local market dynamics. Blackwell's new book provides an especially astute analysis of the European and Asian markets and is a 'must-read' for today's multinational executive."
  —Mark Goldston, president and chief of operations, L.A. Gear, Inc., and author of *The Turnaround Prescription*

"*From the Edge of the World* is a unique and valuable resource for the businessperson who needs to learn to think globally. [Blackwell's] personal anecdotal approach is entertaining and instructive at the same time. A truly insightful book!"
  —Stephanie Shern, partner and national director, Consumer Products Industry Services, Ernst & Young

"I read *From the Edge of the World* with great interest, and . . . I envy [Roger Blackwell] for the opportunity to make these travels. . . . He exhorts American businesspeople to push beyond their normal routine as they view business opportunities inherent in spanning the globe."
  —Frank Wobst, chairman and chief executive officer, Huntington Bancshares Inc.

"Dr. Roger Blackwell's *From the Edge of the World* takes a unique approach to understanding our global neighbors. His anecdotes and learnings about each country, combined with a facts-and-data approach to the monumental changes that have occurred, make this book a must-read for business leaders serious about global marketing."
  —Solomon D. Trujillo, president and chief executive officer, U S WEST Marketing Resources Group, Inc.

# From the Edge of the World

Roger D. Blackwell

Ohio State University Press

*Columbus*

Blackwell, Roger D.
From the edge of the world: Global lessons for personal
and professional prosperity / Roger D. Blackwell.
p. cm.
Includes bibliographical references and index.
ISBN 0–8142–0630–1. — ISBN 0–8142–0631–X (pbk.)
1. Economic history—1990– 2. Social history. I. Title.
HC59.15.B58 1994
330.9—dc20 93–38480
CIP

Text and jacket design by Donna Hartwick.
Type set in ITC Galliard with Bodoni.
Printed by Bookcrafters, Inc., Chelsea, MI.

The paper in this book meets the guidelines for permanence and durability of the Committee on Production Guidelines for Book Longevity of the Council on Library Resources.

9  8  7  6  5  4  3  2  1

# CONTENTS

# PREFACE

**The purpose of this book is to help** create a better, more prosperous lifestyle for readers and to contribute to the survival and prosperity of the businesses in which they work. The method of accomplishing that task is to examine a variety of countries and cultures around the world and see what can be learned in those countries that might be applied to our own situation.

Simply stated, this book contains lessons to be learned from traveling to foreign countries. Some of the lessons learned apply to business firms; others apply to personal and family life; some apply to societal institutions ranging from government to health to schools. With all the learning that I hope occurs from this book, I hope you also have a lot of fun. A verse in Proverbs says that the wise teacher makes learning a joy. I try to do that in this book.

I have met many people around the world to whom I owe much gratitude for teaching me about the globe. It is discouraging to turn on the nightly news and be bombarded with the tragedies of other countries and stories about the wrongdoings of individuals. Because of all the negative publicity the world receives every day and because I am the eternal optimist at heart, I have tried to focus on the positive aspects of the countries I highlight in this book. My hope is that you will read these chapters to learn about the good things to be found around the globe. I know you can read about the bad in most other publications.

After writing nineteen textbooks and research monographs, it is a major departure to write a book such as *Edge*. The book is personal, reflective, succinct, and, I hope, one you will enjoy reading. Most of the textbooks I have written are used in classrooms where students are required to read them. I hope the motivation will be different with this book and that after reading one chapter, you will be anxious to get on to the next.

There is one person without whom this book would not have been written. That person is my wife, Kristina Blackwell. Tina accompanied me on many of the trips described in this book. She and I have discussed most of the topics in the book at length and she has refined my thinking about every one of them. She wrote the chapter on Poland and much of the chapter on Germany and edited or made contributions to all of the other chapters. Throughout the process of the past two years, it was her encouragement that kept the project moving forward. Tina is not only intelligent, personable, and beautiful, she is the most loving spouse any person could ever have.

I would also like to thank Dr. James Ginter and The Ohio State University for facilitating the professional leave that allowed me to travel to the countries I describe in this book. Jim Ginter, as chairman of the Department of Marketing at Ohio State and as a friend, was supportive of not only the professional leave but of many of the other activities that make me probably his most disconcerting faculty member. As chairman, Jim is the one who has to keep answering the question, "Where's Roger and what is he up to now?" Jim is the one who has to respond, "Oh, he is in South Africa (or China, or Peru) and I can only hope he is not starting a revolution someplace."

I am very fortunate to be part of a great institution such as The Ohio State University. I am particularly fortunate to be a part of the marketing department, where I have so many colleagues who truly are excellent teachers and scholars. When parents or executives ask me about sending students to Ohio State, I highly recommend the school, especially the College of Business, which is the area I know best, with sincerity and full confidence that they will receive an excellent education. And at an excellent price!

Many other people had an important part in this book. Ms. Kelley Hughes manages my office and does it well. In addition to preparing manuscripts such as this to be delivered to publishers, she prepares me for my trips, meetings, and classes—and still retains her sanity and disposition. One of the persons who had a great many useful comments that were incorporated into this book was Alfred Stephan, and I appreciate his insightful and timely suggestions. I also thank Trudy Stephan for her help at home and at the office. My parents, Dr. and Mrs. Dale Blackwell, have believed for decades that I could be a good teacher and writer—and apparently still do even after reading the manuscript for this book.

I also appreciate the great support that I received from the Ohio State University Press, especially the director, Peter Givler, and the acquisitions editor, Charlotte Dihoff, who initiated the project on behalf of the OSU Press. I also appreciate the support of Sara Austin in the Office of the President at Ohio State, who read articles I had written in *Business First* and called me to suggest that I expand those ideas and that publishing them would be consistent with President Gordon Gee's belief in a university without walls.

Tom Peters, a friend and inspiration for all professors who believe change can be achieved among business leaders, encouraged me to write a book of this nature. Some of the material in chapter 6 was originally published in his syndicated column when he asked me to be a guest columnist while he was out of the country. Tom Peters, who was once a faculty member at Stanford's Graduate School of Business, sets a very high standard for professors who want to have an impact on society rather than merely study it.

My wife tells me this is a good bathroom book. You can read a few pages, think about them, and read a few more pages another time. Regardless of how—or where—you read this book, I appreciate your taking the time to read it and think about the issues I raise in the following pages. If you have comments or questions, please write me at The Ohio State University. I am serious about the concept of a university without walls and I still believe in the Socratic method.

# 1

# TO THE EDGE OF THE WORLD AND BEYOND

**On a map of the world dated 1297,** the land now known as Europe was shown with considerable detail. Beyond the land mass was blue water. Beyond the water, however, was a line marked "Edge of the World" with a fearful admonition to travelers: "beyond the edge, there be dragons."

For many people in American business, the admonition remained relevant for centuries and continues even today. Never venture beyond the safety of what is known about buying, selling, and working in American markets and corporations. Venturing beyond the borders of the known, meaning domestic, markets was something for only a few citizens and a few business organizations.

Not many Americans ventured beyond the edge. Those who did were not ordinary people. Magnates, movie stars, or perhaps Mafia braved travel beyond the borders of the United States. For the masses, with the possible exception of a summer vacation in

1

Canada or Mexico, traveling—or even the possibility of doing business—in other countries was not even a dream, let alone a reality.

The U.S. military gave the masses the greatest opportunity to explore other countries. For some, those experiences were truly an awakening to new cultures and new markets. For many, probably most, the experiences did not extend much beyond the rice paddies of Vietnam or the PXs and BXs of Germany.

Universities and colleges encouraged students to study abroad. Travel the summer in Europe. Enroll in an exchange program. Get a job and live in another country. Those were often the words of advice of universities and their professors. A few responded to the advice; but as a proportion of the total student body, the fraction who went abroad or believed they could afford such an experience was minute. Even among students, supposedly the most open to new horizons, only a few ventured beyond the edge of the U.S. border.

## *A New Wind Is Blowing*

The resistance to sailing beyond the edge is changing. It changed decades ago for people in countries other than the United States. Soon after World War II, students left their own borders to study in America. Throughout the world, people observed that America was the winner; many people concluded it was also the place to learn how to be a winner. For most Americans, it was also clear that America won in every way—military, money, and the media. Why go anyplace else to learn or to earn?

Those who cared to look, however, could see that the world was changing and that other winners were emerging. The Japanese might have been beaten and they might have been thought once to be producers of cheap, low-quality goods. By the 1980s, however, most Americans had come to quite a different conclusion. In the process, consumers elevated Sony and Honda to the best selling and most respected brands in America. But few Americans had any understanding of the Rising Sun beyond the edge of the world they called the Pacific Ocean. Even fewer Americans spoke the language of Japan, understood its culture, or knew how to penetrate the business barriers built by tightly knit suppliers in a *kereitsu*.

The edge was expanding, it could be argued. During the 1970s and the 1980s, most Americans pushed the edge further out in their minds. Many European and Eurasian countries were allies. By the 1980s, those countries were beginning to be on our map of the known world. We even knew the names of the royalty in England and Monaco, some of the wines of France, the cars of Germany, and the banks of Switzerland!

Some countries, especially India, were neutral, a classification that Americans never did understand. For Americans, the world was either democratic or Communist. A wall definitely put any non-democratic countries beyond the edge of understanding for most Americans. And almost no one expected that wall to fall with the rapidity or impact that it did on that fateful day in November 1989 to usher in the new world of the 1990s. In many ways, the fall of the wall was the prelude to the twenty-first century.

## Fall of the Wall

The fall of the Berlin Wall may well have been the pivotal point in American thinking about global lifestyles, economics, and the marketing and management methods required for survival in the twenty-first century. Perhaps no single event sparked an interest in global markets and broke America's bubble of ethnocentricity as did the announcement that the Berlin Wall would be torn down. Ethnocentricity is a disease that has infected many an American corporation for decades. Focusing only on one's own way of doing things with little sensitivity or interest in the ways of the rest of the world is a common symptom of the disease.

The wall came down and Americans looked beyond the edge of the known world for the first time in half a century. Unlike the sailors of old, most Americans did not see dragons beyond the edge; they assumed that the fall of communism would bring peace and prosperity to the former Communist countries. History books that describe the changes occurring in Eastern European and other formerly Communist countries may some day reveal, however, that there were more dragons lurking in those countries than ever lurked beyond the edge of medieval maps!

The fall of the wall provided a symbolic end to the Cold War that preoccupied Americans for close to a half century. Americans were raised in a culture that taught that communism was the mortal enemy of capitalism. Almost every aspect of national policy was dominated by the Cold War. Much of the industrial complex of the nation—especially research and development investment—was concentrated on supporting the war against communism. Foreign policy decisions were dominated by a process that placed countries into one of two categories—allies or enemies. And the process was usually viewed in a military context, rarely as economic or trading allies or enemies.

For Japan and Germany, the globalization perspective was much different. For the most part, the Japanese had been prohibited from fighting the Cold War, at least as a military power. A little realism about the potential source of military might to fight the Soviet Union encouraged more of a military role for West Germany, but still a diminished role compared to the United States. With the military cold war concentrated between the U.S. and the U.S.S.R., other countries began rebuilding their economic resources to be ready for a more globalized economy.

With the fall of the wall, an astute observer might have paraphrased the ancient philosophy of monarchies by commenting, "The Cold War is over. Long live the Cold War." But a new cold war is being fought on economic principles, and the principal weapons are business strategies and globalized personnel. Companies and countries that win this war will not be those with the most military resources, or even with the most physical and natural resources. The new cold war is thoroughly globalized and will be won by individuals and organizations with the most effective perspectives on global management.

The fall of communism has profound effects in many other countries than those that are considered Communist. One of the most important reasons to be optimistic about the future of African countries is the withdrawal of support from the former Soviet Union and Eastern European countries. Those countries are now focusing more on market systems for progress, which ultimately will contribute to their prosperity, I believe. The collapse of support from Communist countries in Latin America is also a significant force, for both good and bad, as you will read in chapter 13 when we describe Peru. I believe Cuba, North Korea, and other Communist countries will change—with both good and bad effects to be observed in their transition.

## *Empiricism Is Better than Philosophy*

The Berlin Wall came down not because of debate about Marxist-Leninist philosophy, but because of empiricism. Looking across the wall both figuratively and, with the aid of television, literally, East Germans could see that the market system produces ample numbers of consumer goods such as cars and televisions while communism did not. Hardly anyone expected the fall would be so abrupt. Nor did people expect the reverberations to come so soon and be so strong. No longer is the war between communism and capitalism (despite vestiges that remain of that war). Rather, the war today is between various forms of capitalism that might loosely be called the American, the Japanese, and the German versions (Burstein, 1991).

Lester Thurow in his book *Head To Head* (1992) looked at the more than 340 million consumers in the European market and concluded that as the largest market in the world, Europe will do what the country with the largest market historically does. The dominant country will establish the economic and marketing rules for the rest of the world. The General Agreement on Trade and

Tariffs (GATT) has fallen apart for precisely that reason; the United States no longer sets the rules. In the nineteenth century, the British dominated the world and established the rules for the global economy. In the twentieth century, the United States dominated the rules that managers must learn if they operate globally. If Thurow is right in his analysis, management and marketing in the twenty-first century will be dominated by the Europeans, who will be dominated by the large and economically powerful, reunified Germany.

## Capitalistic Diversity

The environment for global business today is one of capitalistic diversity. A monolithic concept of capitalism no longer exists. Even more than the Japanese, American, and European versions, there are variations that are distinctively Dutch, Singaporean, Korean, South African, Middle Eastern, and reflections of other countries.

From the remnants of communism are also found variations of the new blended economies. China and the U.S.S.R. took different paths toward a market economy. The U.S.S.R. changed its political system before changing the economic system. In China, the economic system is changing before the political system is changed. The world is watching to observe which process is better. But both countries depend upon global business to move ahead, and both countries provide opportunities for globalized firms that understand the changes in China, the former Soviet Union, and countries such as Cuba and North Korea in the future.

## Sailing beyond the Edge

Christopher Columbus was one of those early discoverers who was willing to take the risk of sailing beyond the edge. Although by the time Columbus made his historic voyages, it was pretty well known that the world was round, the fear of falling off the edge was real for earlier sailors. In a sense, that analogy applies today.

Few managers, at least among the most competent, believe their firms can exist without going beyond the edge of domestic markets, although few have actually made the voyage. Successful managers increasingly realize that they must be sailors and discoverers of a global world. Managers ready to captain their ships into the twenty-first century must understand the boundaries, the cultures, the economies, and the businesses of countries throughout the world.

Many people are not managers, of course, nor do they aspire to that position. Other than intellectual curiosity, why should they care much about what lies beyond the edge of their own world? Many people want only to live quiet lives in their own part of the world, raising their families, receiving decent incomes, and doing their jobs well. Unfortunately, it is increasingly possible that they may have no jobs if they and their companies do not understand how to compete in a global economy.

It might seem an alarmist view to assert that everyone must understand what lies beyond the edge of the national boundary in order to survive in the future. It is not an exaggeration, however, to say that few firms can exist without a global perspective. Some observers believe that as many as 40 percent of Americans will have no permanent career opportunity if they do not understand and develop global skills. And it is safe to say that no person should be considered for promotion to a position of major responsibility in any organization (profit or nonprofit) unless that person can think globally. For those reasons, in the final chapter of the book we will describe what it means to think globally and the kind of perspectives, skills, and strategies required to survive in the global economy that lies "beyond the edge" of the domestic economy.

## *Beyond the Edge*

Unlike on the maps of the ancient world, there are no dragons waiting beyond the edge to devour roving sailors. There are rough waters between the United States and some of these countries, and occasionally there are hostile local inhabitants. Mostly, however, there are only increased riches to be discovered for both the guests and the hosts.

I believe every person should travel to and learn from as many other countries as possible. Unfortunately, for most people few, if any, visits to other countries are possible. Closing the gap between the desirability of personally traveling to many countries and the economic reality of doing so was the genesis of this book. That is why I describe it as "lessons learned" from the edge of the world. The lessons are ones that I have learned, and I hope that many of them will be useful for your own thinking. Reading the book and learning whatever lessons you find relevant is, at least, a lot cheaper than making all the voyages yourself!

## *Universities without Walls*

As a professor at the nation's largest residential university, I was assigned the task of teaching a new course on global marketing. Our faculty wanted the best preparation possible for students so that they would know how to survive and thrive in the global economy that we all foresaw on the horizon. To prepare for the class, the university granted me a one-year leave of absence. Along with collecting and analyzing data and reading and writing for academic journals, I decided to travel to many areas of the world—to go beyond the edge of normal preparation to teach.

I recognized that our students needed as much insight as possible into the realities of the global culture and economy. Textbooks are useful, but they're no substitute for experiencing a culture firsthand—talking to people, observing how businesses

8

market and manage, eating local food, and surviving on local streets and highways. With the assistance of IBM and some other business firms (and by using up a decade of accumulated frequent-flier mileage), I spent a year collecting materials for the new global marketing course at The Ohio State University.

A university without walls is the proper description of The Ohio State University and other great public institutions. Thus, I was asked how people other than our students could benefit from my year of study. Textbooks and journal articles are the normal outlets for research and ones in which I have published for many years. But how could we bring the insights, anecdotes, and experiences I was gaining to a wider audience?

Some friends in the American Marketing Association asked me if I would write a column for the local chapter's newsletter describing what marketers should know about some of the countries I was studying. I did and when the column was shown to editors of *Business First*, they asked to publish the column periodically in expanded form. The response was very positive, and I received many requests for columns about specific countries. Bringing the columns together in updated and expanded form was the foundation for this book.

Tom Peters, author of *Search for Excellence* and other best selling books, also asked me to write a column for him while he was out of the country. Lessons learned from the Netherlands were the subject of that column, syndicated in many newspapers by the *Chicago Tribune*. The Dutch lessons in profitability are the basis of chapter 4 in this book.

The countries about which I have written are not necessarily the most important, although they are, in some respects, among the most useful analytically and are prototypical of other countries. I have not yet traveled much to Eastern Europe, a void I hope to correct in the future. Thus, to fill the void in my coverage of those areas, I asked my wife, Kristina Blackwell, to write about Poland. She is my coauthor in our textbook *Contemporary Cases in Consumer Behavior* (published by Dryden division of Harcourt Brace

Jovanovich in 1993) and wrote many of the global cases in that book. Chapter 6 is written by Tina and reflects her experiences in that country with her father, Alfred Stephan, who served as interpreter for her in Poland.

I have tried to keep chapters on each country as brief as possible. I tried to be succinct in my writing. My purpose was not to answer all the questions or document all the opinions as textbooks might do. My purpose was to stimulate questions in your own mind that might lead to your own research, thoughtful questioning, and perhaps to visiting the countries I write about.

I could have written about many more countries and would have liked to do so. If the book had been much longer, however, you might not have been willing to buy it or read it!

## *What You Get When You Read This Book*

I wrote this book much more personally than the textbooks I normally write. After all, most people find textbooks pretty boring. Even mine! I decided to approach the chapters in this book in a personal, brisk, and—I hope—enticing style. I want you to experience many of the observations, insights, and feelings I did as I visited each country. Most of all, I want to share ideas that I discovered in my global journey that you can apply to help yourself and your business prosper.

When I returned from trips, I was often asked questions about what I had learned. Sometimes I appeared on radio or TV talk shows discussing topics that related to various countries. More often, I found myself in situations where people asked me face-to-face about the countries I visited. They wanted to know about the people in each country, the business environment, and what lessons might be applied to our own situation in the United States or Canada, or in other countries where I visited.

In the seminars I teach for business executives, the question and answer sessions sometimes went into the wee morning hours with discussion of how principles and opportunities from other countries might be applied to the profitability challenges facing North American firms. In my classes at Ohio State and other schools where I have lectured, students often asked questions about how people behave in other countries. Most of the students had never visited these countries, and perhaps thought they would never be able to do so. Often questions came from ordinary people who work in offices and factories who asked about how ordinary people live in other countries and how they solve the problems of food, housing, and economics that face everyone.

Usually my answers did not focus on the physical things in other countries. Generally, I tried to focus on the concepts, principles, and lessons to be learned in other countries. People seemed to be interested in my ideas and conclusions, especially how they might apply to our conditions in North America. Not everyone agreed with me, but most seemed to be stimulated to think about our own situations and problems, sometimes with a new perspective. Quite often someone would comment, "This is interesting. You ought to write your ideas down in a book." So, I did!

Simply stated, the purpose of this book is to invite you to sail with me to distant ports and to learn together what will be helpful in surviving and thriving in the twenty-first century.

2

# BRUSSELS

*Capital of the World?*

**If you are serious about understanding** global business, one country and one city are a must to visit. The country is Belgium. The city is Brussels. With just a little stretch of the imagination, it might be called the new capital of the world.

The nineteenth century was the era of the British Empire. The twentieth century belonged to the United States. But the beginning of the twenty-first century probably will belong to the Europeans, especially the European Community or EC.

### The European Community

In 1993 (technically December 31, 1992), many of the trade barriers that separated twelve European countries came tumbling down. The Who didn't celebrate the event as they did the fall of the Berlin

# BRUSSELS
### *Capital of the World?*

The new symbol of "We Europeans"

Wall, and there may have been less ceremony overall, but the effects are probably far greater.

In Brussels, I spent much of my time in the library and publications offices. There you will find the fascinating details of why Europe is more important as a market than the United States.

The EC is a market of about 380 million people now that the members of the European Free Trade Association (EFTA) have effectively been added to the 337 million already in the EC. The EC is an economy with buying power 50 percent greater than the United States. By the year 2000, experts believe the increase in buying power in the EC will be greater than the current gross domestic product of the United States. If you add in Eastern Europe and the former U.S.S.R, which EC members will probably dominate in marketing, the European market is 850 million people. In this new environment, the United States is a minor league member of world markets.

# BRUSSELS
## *Capital of the World?*

## *Who Gets To Set the Rules for World Trade?*

When you dominate the world, as the United States did in the twentieth century, you get to write the rules for the rest of the world. That is why everyone came to Bretton Woods, New Hampshire, after World War II and signed the GATT agreements. But when you are no longer the world's major market, you no longer get to write the rules. That is one of the reasons that GATT agreements are falling apart. The GATT agreements served a useful purpose. Now we live in a new world of regional trading blocks—with the EC as the largest. The EC will get to write the rules, to define the level playing field that Americans say they want.

The new rules of Europe are designed, among other things, to create a "Fortress Europe" against the Japanese. Europeans, frankly, are afraid the Japanese will do to the European auto, steel, and other industries what they have done to American industries. The Europeans have a plan to prevent that, and the plan is called the EC. In the goals of the EC, the Europeans intend to limit Japanese cars to 14 percent of the total in 2000.

What is the Japanese counterplan? Build in the United States and avoid counting U.S. production as part of the 14 percent limit. In effect, the Japanese hope to let Americans fight the battle of imports because they believe the Europeans fear the Americans less. Why is this of such vital concern to the United States and Canada? Just go to the Honda plant in Marysville, Ohio, and all the supporting businesses in the area. When you see the manufacturing plants for components and subassembly parts in North America, you will quickly observe the importance of understanding the new rules of Europe.

To learn the new rules, you have to look to Brussels. Keep in mind that officially the goal of the EC is political unity—a new nation called the House of Europe. If it were not for that official goal, the EC would be a violation of the GATT agreement. So officially, the EC is a forerunner of a unified political entity. But that is not

The House of the European Community

what people really believe will happen, especially since the Danish referendum voted no on the Maastricht treaty to launch a common European currency and common foreign policy, and the French referendum squeaked by with a plurality of *oui*.

## National Identities?

The national identities of France, Germany, and the others are not going to disappear. Just the opposite. I concluded that political unity is not likely to happen in the near future if ever, but economic cooperation is a reality. Sometimes the media and others minimized the impact of the EC because of the Maastricht mess, but don't forget that on January 1, 1993, more than four hundred trade barriers in Europe fell. Transport trucks now rush more or less freely across what used to be endless waits and costs at the borders of each country.

## *Ignore EC at the Peril of Your Job!*

Margaret Thatcher thought she could ignore Brussels. She lost her job. When the world woke up on January 1, 1993, it was in a world in which any European bank can place an office in any other European city without government permission. Corporations and individuals can borrow from the country with the lowest interest rates, which means that interest rates will eventually be the same throughout Europe and will set the standard for the rest of the world. Mrs. Thatcher threatened to take England out of that system, but to do so would have meant the end of London's financial institutions. It was cheaper to get a new prime minister than to lose one of England's few remaining global economic strengths.

Most Americans can learn from Mrs. Thatcher. Ignore the Common Market at the peril of your job. American firms that have significant sales in Europe had better learn how to operate in Fortress Europe. Make no mistake about the purpose of the EC. First and foremost it is to protect European firms from competition from firms outside Europe. They don't really believe Americans are that effective at competing, but the Europeans sincerely respect (fear) the Japanese. That is one of the primary reasons for Fortress Europe.

The Europeans hope to avoid some of the problems of Japanese competition that plagued the United States in the 1980s. The Americans decided to meet Japanese competition by becoming more productive and have made substantial progress toward that goal. The Europeans must also become more productive, a difficult task considering their high wage rates and social welfare benefits. To a large extent, they are trying to solve their productivity problems by erecting protectionist trade barriers.

16

## *Fears for the Future*

The success of the EC is its biggest problem. In addition to the current twelve countries, enough other countries have applied or expressed interest to bring the total to twenty-six countries. But the original twelve cannot accept the other, mostly poor countries on the same terms. There would be no problem accepting Switzerland (except perhaps on the part of Switzerland, which still savors its neutrality); but the rich EC nations, such as Germany and France, recognize they cannot admit the poor nations on equal terms of currency, pollution, and other items. They already have enough problems with existing poor nations such as Turkey and Greece. The rich nations do not want to—probably cannot—give subsidies to make up the difference in poor countries.

An even bigger fear is the migration from poor countries to rich countries that can exist under EC open market conditions. In the United States we have an "American Community" in which people living in poor states such as Wyoming and Alabama are allowed freely to migrate to Ohio or California. What if we had a "Community of the Americas" in which people from countries such as Mexico or Haiti or Brazil could move to good employment areas in any state?

That analogy illustrates some of the fears that are developing that will limit the ability to assimilate all European countries into the EC. Germany is highly visible for its problem with immigrants, especially the asylum seekers who receive excellent health, education, and income benefits just by moving to Germany. But Belgium, the Netherlands, and other rich European countries have a similar problem. I share the opinion of observers who believe that migration of poor people from Eastern Europe and elsewhere may be the single biggest problem facing the EC.

## *The Maastricht Mess*

How should we interpret the recent referendum in Denmark in which the people rejected approval of the Treaty of Maastricht that would ratify the current structure of the EC? In my judgment, the effects will not be great. Denmark will not withdraw from the EC and its current structure.

A positive vote would have permitted implementing all of the administrative structure of the EC. The vote in Denmark should be interpreted, I believe, as a vote against the bureaucracy that developed in the EC. Not only in Denmark, but in other EC countries, people are rebelling against the development of an administrative bureaucracy that is not politically accountable. They are also rejecting an economy that depends on a unified currency for Europe.

Because the French referendum was so equivocal, the EC bureaucracy will have to be changed substantially. If only Denmark rejected the Maastricht treaty, an accommodation would probably be worked out with little effect. The most important result of current developments is to send a signal that people in Europe still want democracy rather than an administrative bureaucracy. They also want their own currencies, at least for the foreseeable future.

## "We Europeans"

When you visit Brussels, you see evidence everywhere of the reality of the new EC. Buildings, headquarters of international firms that hope to do business in Europe, statistical monographs, and books printed in all the official languages. (Thanks to the United Kingdom, English is one of them!) But throughout Europe, you see other evidence of the new importance of the EC.

When you travel between countries, the most predominant feature of the border signs is the twelve-nation logo of the EC with the host country's name in small print at the bottom. When I used to travel in Europe, I heard people say, "We French . . . ," or "We Germans . . ." Now, more and more, I hear people say, "We Europeans . . ."

Do not conclude that the French will no longer be French and the Germans will no longer be German in terms of culture. Cultural identities of nations are often exaggerated when they are threatened.

The European identity is being layered over national identities. Manufacturers are displaying the EC logo on packages to identify the ability to be sold in any of the countries without tariffs and barriers. The logo can also be found on sweat shirts, T-shirts, Christmas ornaments, and even chocolates! Most signs are now in visual language to overcome the major barrier left in Europe—language.

## *"An American in Europe"*

*An American in Paris* was a great movie years ago. In the future, the typical American firm and its employees will have to be more concerned with how to operate in the EC—how to be "An American in Europe."

If a standard is set by the EC to apply to product specifications or labeling, then all firms in EC countries must abide by that standard, including American firms serious about selling in Europe. Many U.S. firms will find that the standards were deliberately set to be different from Japanese or American standards; this will initially serve as an effective trade barrier.

But if there is no EC standard, then the standards of one EC country must be accepted in all the other countries of the EC. For example, if there is no EC standard for ingredients in beer, then French beer can legally be sold in Germany without meeting the normal German standards. And German or Swiss cheeses can be sold in France without meeting the normal standards for making Brie cheese in France. As you can guess, this is going to make for some pretty heated arguments over the next few months and years.

For an American firm, the meaning is more ominous. As a result of what the EC calls the Single Market Initiative (SMI), a German firm and a French firm will be on equal footing when selling to an Italian or British firm. But an American firm will not. Unless the American firm has an EC subsidiary that produces the product, the American firm must continue to meet the idiosyncratic and usually expensive rules of each nation.

For executives of American firms that fail to understand what it takes to compete in the new Europe, the future may be as traumatic as it was for Maggie Thatcher, who couldn't come to grips with the reality that if you are not in the EC in the future, you have not much of a future in the largest market in the world.

Reciprocity is sometimes offered as an answer to the Fortress Europe goal of the EC. A U.S. firm could operate in Europe but only if the U.S. grants the same rights to European firms as those of the EC. For example, Bank One could open in Europe and operate freely but only if the U.S. grants reciprocal (and identical) rights to EC banks. As long as a single state restricts interstate banking or the federal rules restrict U.S. banks from owning and managing other corporations (a practice encouraged in Europe, for example), we would not be meeting the definition of reciprocity. American banks, therefore, could not operate under the same rules or play on a level playing field.

In the 1980s and early 1990s, there was great optimism about the future of the European Community. After Maastricht, observers became much more pessimistic. This "bearishness" on the EC was accentuated by the worldwide economic slowdown and problems with currency and interest rates, leading to what was often referred to as "Eurosclerosis." The inability or wisdom (depending on your viewpoint) of the EC to deal with Yugoslavia, Bosnia, and related issues caused many people to write off the EC as unimportant.

Don't do that! The EC, despite its problems, is one of the most important developments that will influence the twenty-first century. If you do not understand the EC and the rest of the European nations who want into the "Club," you will have a difficult time in the future managing a company in the United States or perhaps keeping a job in most North American companies.

# BRUSSELS
## *Capital of the World?*

### *A Sweet City*

Brussels is not a city of great beauty or culture compared to other European capitals. Its economic growth has been among the highest in Europe but is mostly tied to establishment of bureaucratic offices associated with the EC and with offices of firms that need to interact with the EC. Brussels is a government and service city more than a manufacturing city. In that sense, it is much like Columbus, Ohio, or other cities that combine the advantages of being a government headquarters, a business service formation center and an academic community.

There is one product that the Belgians manufacture well, probably better than anyone in the world. The product—chocolates. The Swiss and the French make good chocolates too, but nobody does it better than the Belgians. Neuhaus is possibly the best of the major brands in Belgium, although I prefer to walk down the streets of Brussels and sample the homemade products of small family shops. Godiva is the best known brand of premium Belgian chocolate in the world. Probably less known is the fact that Godiva is now a wholly owned subsidiary of the Campbell Soup Company! Kind of spoils the image, doesn't it?

A trip to Brussels is essential for understanding the future of global business. It is a hustling, bustling city that in many ways reminds me of Washington. Bureaucrats. Office buildings. Influence seekers. Peddlers. And good food, good chocolates, and great Belgian waffles.

That's the way I see it, looking past the edge.

# 3

# JAPAN

## *Clouds Cross the Rising Sun*

**Perhaps no country evokes as many** mixed reactions as Japan. People alternate between Japan worshiping and Japan bashing. Some observers speak of Japan as the model of family values, efficiency, total quality management, lifetime employment, long-range planning, and marketing sophistication. Other observers blame Japan for everything from the unemployment of American workers to the bankruptcies of American firms. The Japan bashers often accuse Japanese firms of dumping products abroad and cite artificial trade barriers aimed at keeping American firms out of Japanese markets as the reasons for American difficulty in selling to Japan.

Japan bashing became a popular sport during the 1992 presidential campaign, highlighted—or lowlighted, perhaps—by the trip of President George Bush to Japan. Not only did he lead a delegation of auto executives and others who joined the outcry against Japan, but President Bush succumbed to the flu, suffering the

22

The future of Japan—its children

indignity of public regurgitation in front of television cameras beaming the process to the entire world.

I did not catch the flu in Japan and was not accompanied by a host of highly paid chief executive officers, but I did observe some trends that may be helpful in putting Japan in perspective. Understanding Japan can be very useful in thinking about America's competitive problems and the probability of solving them.

Many observers have reported some of the reasons that firms have been successful in the Land of the Rising Sun. But we may yet see a sunset on the horizon. Before we rush either to emulate or eliminate the Japanese, however, we need to realize that some of the Japanese advantages, such as lifetime employment and "workaholism," will eventually become disadvantages.

## *Ginza Is Much More than a TV Knife*

The most striking characteristic of Japan perhaps is the concentration of so many people in so little space. The latest census was re-

23

An exclusive office supply store

leased during my trip indicating Japan's official population of 123 million in a land area the size of Montana. About 70 percent of the land is mountains, leaving most people packed together in small homes dependent for mobility on small cars and motor scooters or on the highly efficient mass transit system.

The scarcity of land has produced real estate values that are almost incomprehensible. Before the recent recession, land was selling for $248,000 per square meter in the Ginza area, site of Tokyo's most exclusive shopping. Shopping—which happens to be a favorite pastime for me and my wife—in the Ginza district is wonderful as long as you don't take your wallet. Then it can be downright dangerous.

Someone calculated that the land on which the Imperial Palace is located is more valuable than the total amount of all real estate in California! One of my Canadian friends told me half seriously that the Canadians, who have a large embassy in Tokyo, are considering selling it and renting much smaller space. By selling the land, the Canadians could pay off nearly half of their national debt. Maybe the United States should consider a similar plan!

## *Dinner for Four: $1,000*

High real estate values are one reason that everything is very expensive in Japan. Not only land costs are involved. Food costs are sky high. My wife and I ate often at the Sizzler near Shinjuku station in Tokyo because the all-you-can-eat salad buffet was only twenty dollars a meal. After surviving for days on rice—not being a sushi fan— my wife was pleased to eat something that crunched when chewed. American business executives moan that a business dinner for four at a top Japanese restaurant can easily add up to one thousand dollars on the credit card.

Food costs are astronomical partly because of the small farms that dominate Japanese agriculture. Seven levels of distribution through wholesalers and retailers, compared to three in the United States, also add to the costs. A major weakness in Japan's competitive situation is its distribution system; it is an opportunity for global competitors with more efficient approaches to distribution.

## *Postage-Stamp Farms*

Farms are postage-stamp-size plots smaller than most suburban lawns in the United States. The small plots are intensively farmed by a single family for generations. When you see the minuscule size of Japanese farms, it is easy to understand why the rice farmers of Japan are so vehement, and sometimes violent, about allowing low-cost rice to be imported into Japan. To do so would destroy the lifestyle of millions of farm families, a lifestyle so fundamental to

Japanese philately: Postage-stamp farms where each small parcel of land supports an entire family

Japan that it cannot be allowed to happen. The farms cover Japan, providing green islands of produce in the suburbs and throughout the countryside. The small farms, and the small family-owned retail shops that operate on the same principles, are important reasons why the Japanese unemployment rate historically has been around 1 or 2 percent until recently.

Understanding the dependence on small (really small!) farms that have provided a family's living for generations is a key to understanding why Japan cannot allow many agricultural imports, even though the cost of imported products might be one-tenth the cost of domestic agricultural products. Allowing inexpensive American rice into Japan, in the way the United States has allowed (originally) inexpensive Japanese cars into America, cannot happen when the tables are turned. For the Japanese to lower their trade barriers on agricultural products would literally topple the government. Not only will American farmers not be selling as much as they would like, Japanese consumers will continue to pay artificially high food prices compared to what would exist without trade barriers.

## *From Low Costs to High Quality*

Soaring costs have placed the Japanese in a difficult predicament in competing with other countries of the world. Japan won much of its market share in the seventies and early eighties by being a low-cost producer. Today Japan must compete on dimensions other than cost, and generally it does. To a major extent, however, the Japanese economy has become vulnerable to the low costs of catch-up economies such as in Korea, Malaysia, and now China.

Two consequences ensue from the threatened Japanese cost structure. First, the Japanese will fight trade wars mostly on the basis of quality and market orientation rather than cost. American business will do well to understand the nature of this problem. We are not losing the trade wars because of lower costs in Japan or "dumping" practices, even though they occasionally exist.

We simply do not build cars that the Japanese want to buy, even without trade barriers. The often-mentioned example is that Americans try only to sell cars with the steering wheel on the left side, which is often the wrong side. Some Detroit leaders have replied that if the Japanese would guarantee a certain volume of imports, Americans would adapt the steering wheels. Can you recall, however, the American government guaranteeing Japanese firms any minimum levels when they decided to enter U.S. markets?

That reveals the fundamental problem Americans face when selling to Japan. It is a problem that limits Americans when they compete in the rest of the world as well.

The problem? We are ethnocentric. We expect people to learn our language in order to buy our products. We expect them to change their distribution system to fit our way of doing business. We expect people who are accustomed to high quality in products to accept our lower quality standards.

Some American firms are successful in Japan—IBM, Boeing, Tyson Chicken, Toys R Us, and McDonald's to name just a few. Until American executives learn Japanese, understand the Japanese culture, target products that fit the size and economics of Japan and produce products of high quality, we are only misleading ourselves (or are our politicians misleading us?) about how to win the trade war in which we are engaged with Japan.

The greatest trade barriers faced by American firms are not political ones enacted by the government, although some of those do exist. The greatest barrier is the language! Nearly every Japanese executive stationed in the United States learns passable English, but it is rare for American executives to know Japanese. We probably won't be taken seriously about selling to Japan until we do. High school students in places such as Dublin, Ohio (which is near a Honda plant in Marysville), who learn Japanese may be part of our best hope for saving American jobs.

## From Mine Sweepers to Transpacific Jets

A second consequence of the rising challenge to Japanese economic success is more ominous. The Japanese are increasingly under economic attack from other Pacific Rim countries, especially Korea and China. Eventually Japan will have to have more than a defensive force in order to protect its economic interests, at least in the Pacific Rim.

A first step in the remilitarization of Japan was sending mine sweepers to the Gulf War, at the encouragement of the United States. Another step was changing the Japanese constitution to permit sending Japanese troops to foreign locations (such as the Krill Islands) for defensive purposes.

Japan needs new industries to fuel its falling economic growth. The obvious next target is the aerospace and airframe business, an industry that the United States has dominated since World War II. The present Japanese airframe business is embryonic, but it may increase mightily in the next few years. It was inhibited in the past, due to the lack of military/defense industries. That will change, I believe, partly because Japan must protect its economic interests in the Pacific Rim and needs a military capability. Changes will also occur because Americans will be unlikely to fight in places such as Vietnam and Kuwait to protect Japanese economic interests.

The United States dictated terms following World War II. The U.S.-imposed constitution prohibited Japan from being a military power. In return, the United States pledged to be Japan's protector. But that commitment is changing. As a result, not only will the Japanese probably become one of the major military powers (along with Germany for similar reasons), but the Japanese will provide serious competition to Boeing and many other military and commercial industries. By the end of the decade, we may be flying a Toyota across the Pacific!

## *Lights at Night in Tokyo Skyscrapers*

Anyone walking around Tokyo at night can see a key reason for Japanese success. Look up and you will see skyscrapers with all the offices lighted. The lights are on because the workers are still there.

Japanese firms succeed not because they are smarter than Americans but partly because their managers work longer hours. Although their managers arrive at work about the same time as do Americans, Tokyo office buildings are shining bright as late as 10 or 11 P.M.

At midnight, subways are full of blue-suited, white-shirted, attaché-toting managers on their way home from work (and often from a little socializing with other workers). Six days a week this occurs, although they may leave earlier on Saturday. Holidays are few and vacations, although earned, are usually not taken. I visited Japan during a holiday and the hospitals reported an increase in admissions for depression, nausea, and headaches. The cause? Those are the symptoms of employees who are not permitted to go to work because of vacations or holidays!

The Japanese work ethic (at the expense of family life for male managers) has given Japanese firms a big edge over U.S. firms. Eventually, though, I believe it will destroy them. A recent survey showed that Japanese fathers knew only three of their children's friends. The same survey showed that Japanese women have such low regard for their husbands that they respond well to cosmetic ads that describe husbands as "cockroaches." The survey reported that the dream for most Japanese women was an American husband. (No comment about the validity of their belief!)

Ample evidence suggests that the younger generation of Japanese workers dislikes the work ethic of their elders. Potentially, it may change. Young people visibly reject the long hours, working on Saturdays, and business golf for thirty-six holes on Sunday. Their rejection of previous work patterns may eventually dilute some of the Japanese advantage.

One reason Japan has such an extensive night life is the small homes in which nearly every family, even affluent ones, must live. Therefore, business entertainment must usually be outside the home. The young people have no place to entertain friends, especially those of the opposite sex. Thus, "love hotels" are common, with rooms rented by the hour.

Japan has lots of bars. One study indicates that 82 percent of all Japanese bars are karaoke bars. More than 6 million people sing in karaoke bars every day (or night). Americans are beginning to emulate the Japanese but to a much lesser extent. The last time I visited Bourbon Street in New Orleans, I did note, somewhat sadly, that a karaoke bar was attracting more visitors than the jazz clubs that dominated the street historically. It is just one more example of Americans learning from the Japanese, I suppose.

## *Live Five Years Longer: Be Japanese!*

American citizens and business leaders have much to learn from the Japanese, such as their cultural empathy and ability to learn our language, emphasis on quality, relentless pursuit of market segments, belief by both managers and workers in the need to help the corporation succeed, and willingness to accept long-term commitments and payoffs. Those cultural traits have given the Japanese much more of an edge than their trade barriers.

Anyone in the United States can also learn much from the healthy lifestyle of the Japanese: they live an average of five years longer than we do. The reason is probably obvious when looking for a diet drink in a Japanese restaurant. They are hard to find because it is hard to find a person in Japan who needs to lose weight. Perhaps the reason obesity is so rare is the low-fat diet most people eat. Or maybe the answer is simpler: the food costs too much to be able to eat too much! Whatever the reason, the average Japanese lives five years longer than the average American. Maybe the answer is that hard work is healthy!

## *The Purpose of Government*

Perhaps the most important lesson Americans can learn by visiting Japan is to understand a system in which the government believes its very existence is dependent upon helping business thrive. It is part of the constitution. Government's primary purpose is to help business!

Helping business is not the highest purpose of the American government. In fact, it often seems the opposite. In the United States's form of capitalism, the role of government is the regulator—to protect consumers from big, bad business. Even the media often portray business as something bad.

That is not the way things are in Japan. The best students go to law school—really a kind of government service program rather than the litigious process taught in American law schools. The best students in all of Japan go to Tokyo University and the very best of those go into government service, probably to MITI, the government agency to encourage business trade.

# JAPAN
### Clouds Cross the Rising Sun

One thing is clear if you are a businessperson in Japan. When you sit down with a government leader, that person is more intelligent that you are. That might not always be true in the United States!

Early in the history of the United States, Noah Webster pointed out a basic fact. If a country imports more than it exports, the people in the country will always be poor. The Japanese government understands the advice of that American just as they understand the advice of another American, Edward Deming, whose principles of quality management permeate business. And the Japanese organize all of government and society accordingly.

At the same time we admire their success, we can learn from the problems that face the Japanese. Japan has placed so much emphasis on industrial goods that the typical citizen has relatively few consumer goods. Typically, the Japanese live in small homes, commute two to three hours a day, are rarely able to drive cars except on Sundays, are required to get a permit from the police department to buy a new car (documenting they have a valid parking space), have what most Americans would consider a miserable family life, and blatantly discriminate against women.

In all the discussions about losing jobs to Japan, few voices seem to speak out for consumers in America. It is tragic to see Americans lose jobs but it is also important to realize that we have the cheapest cars—and just about every other product—in the world.

Clothing, food, and many other items are 20 to 30 percent lower in the United States than in other industrialized countries because we have lower tariffs. Which is worse, to have thousands of highly paid auto workers lose their jobs or to have the other 240 million consumers pay thousands more for their cars? When all is said and done, I believe most Americans have a better lifestyle than most Japanese, even though Japan has the highest per capita average income in the world.

Do politicians or others help anyone by Japan bashing? Are we really losing our competitive battles and employees' jobs because of

Japan's trade barriers? Do we need presidents leading trade missions to Japan? The answer is, "Probably not."

The real tragedy will occur, in my judgment, if we blame trade barriers as the cause for our diminished competitiveness in America. To do so often causes American workers and managers to fail to address the real issues—product quality, segmentation, service and customer satisfaction, cultural empathy, and an understanding by most citizens that a government that fails to help business succeed eventually creates a nation that fails.

That's the way I see it . . . from the edge.

# 4

# GERMANY

*The New Management Example*

**Sausage, sauerkraut, and beer are probably** what most of us think about when we think of Germany. Those a little more daring might want to test their German pronunciation of words such as *Streuselkuchen, Schweinebraten,* and *Spaetzle.* Needless to say, all of these things are *wunderbar.*

But there is more to Germany than what you might find at an Americanized Oktoberfest—strangely held in September. My understanding of the country and its people has expanded in recent years not only because of the firms with which I've been privileged to work, but because of my wife's family. Talking with them late at night, after a ceremonial serving of Jaegermeister, is one way to learn about the concerns of citizens of all ages and economic backgrounds. They have told me about their triumphs, their views of world affairs, and the state of the family unit. They have concerns about their youth just as we do; gangs have become a universal problem.

# GERMANY
## *The New Management Example*

Winter tranquility in Bavaria's Straubing

Many factors work together to make one culture different from another. Germany is no exception, although its predicament might be more complex because of political and personal sensitivities following World War II that will never disappear. The question is, How will Germany fare in the next century? What will its role be in the changing world order? Will it be assertive enough to make unpopular changes for the good of the country?

## *A Chip Off the Old Wall*

Ethnocentricity is a disease that has infected many an American corporation for decades. Focusing only on our own way of doing things with little sensitivity or interest in the ways of the rest of the world is the most common symptom of the disease. Working with various companies around the world in the area of global marketing has allowed me to peer "over the edge" into management forms and styles that are the direction of the future. Germany is one of the most important destinations for American managers to search for perspectives from the leading edge.

Perhaps no single event sparked an interest in global markets and broke the bubble of ethnocentricity as did the announcement that the Berlin Wall would be torn down. The Berlin Wall came down, not because of debate about Marxist-Leninist philosophy. The wall came down because of empiricism. East Germans looked across the wall figuratively and, with the aid of television, literally, and saw that the free market system produces ample numbers of telephones and cars, while communism does not.

I watched with my family as we saw the first East Germans cross the border into the west. Some came in cars, some on foot, many of them carrying everything they owned into the land of opportunity. For me it was a time of amazement; for my wife's family it was one of tears and joy for the strangers they watched and lost family they prayed for.

The fall of the wall caused many American business executives to see something very clearly, namely, the rise of Germany as an emerging global superpower. The European Community (EC) may or may not dominate world markets but Germany will dominate the EC. Currently, the German government is investing many billions of marks a year in infrastructure in eastern Germany. The costs of reunification, which are primarily to equalize benefits of the social welfare system western Germans have enjoyed for decades, are huge but the process is well under way.

The fall of the wall also signified what few believed would happen as rapidly as it has—the collapse of communism as a serious economic model. If the world exists centuries from now, it appears likely that communism will be little more than a footnote in history textbooks stating, "It was an economic system that was tried briefly during the twentieth century and failed."

## *Ein Ziel*

Countries often rise to power or greatness because their people are inspired by a common goal, *ein Ziel*. Truly great leaders create a vision for their nation, that vision often being an optimistic dream.

After World War II the *Ziel* for the Germans was to rebuild their country and regain their position as an economic power. They had to prove once again to themselves and to the rest of the world that, although they were down, they were not out. It was their ambition and vision that propelled them to the top in less than forty years, ranking Germany among the highest countries in the world in per capita income and quality of life.

Sometime during the 1980s, Germans started to look to their leaders for a new *Ziel*. The Germans were no longer satisfied with dreaming of a few points of economic growth. Their thoughts had extended over the wall to their brothers in the east. But the vision extends onward to Eastern Europe and eventually Russia. They dreamed of East Germany being the gateway to the untapped Eastern European market.

And the dream came true. I remember watching CNN coverage of the related events. It caused me to wonder what *Ziel* America has. What is our common vision? What will it take to unite us to have such a vision? In America, we no longer have the Cold War to unite people in a common cause. Do we need a new enemy?

## *Hey Brother, Can You Spare a Mark?*

My wife's grandmother had a dream, as did many Germans who remembered one Germany. It was to reunite a people who had been separated by a stone wall. The reunification of East and West Germany poses challenges as well as opportunities for both sides. The East Germans had for years seen the prosperity enjoyed by their brothers and sisters in the West, thereby making the East German market one that was ready to explode with the desire to buy.

East Germany can be characterized as 17 million people with the need and desire to buy everything. Under communist rule they experienced the ability to buy goods, but lacked available goods to buy. Since reunification they lack many of the resources needed to satiate their appetite for goods, but they are willing to work to gain resources to spend. As East Germans enter the West German work force and as businesses are developed in East Germany, they are rapidly becoming a large, viable market for almost any type of product.

After the elation surrounding reunification died down, the economic realities of the event started to settle in. I was with a group of friends during some of Germany's periods of questioning and doubts of the effects of the union. I asked them if they felt reunification would translate into a liability or an opportunity for Germany. They quickly asked me how much time I had to discuss the answer. In retrospect my question was equivalent to a child asking a parent why the earth is round.

They told me it all depended on the frame of reference. They were used to taking a long-term rather than short-term view. It is not certain how much money West Germany will have to invest in East Germany in the form of economic aid, but the investment will surely have a high return in the long run. The group of business leaders said they would—at least out of obligation—give East Germans jobs, training, housing, and currency. But it would not be an easy task to ask workers to sacrifice pay raises and housing for strangers.

But even with expenditures by the government and business, the West German economy is able to add East Germany's $200 billion gross national product to its trillion-dollar annual output, thereby increasing the distance from Europe's other economic leaders, France and Great Britain. Germany also gained 17 million citizens to be 78 million people strong, while Italy and Great Britain remain at 58 million and 57 million citizens, respectively.

## *Reunification and Rebuilding*

My friends summarized the opportunities presented by reunification in two ways. First, Germany would get a new supply of labor. Second, Germany would have a gateway to the east.

German companies have imported foreign labor, primarily through Turkish and Slavic guest workers, for many years. However, problems stemming from cultural differences have caused unrest among German management as well as German citizens. Therefore, the idea of replacing the Turkish workers with eastern German workers excites most German companies. Eastern German workers demand more in wages than the foreign workers of the past; but the education, literacy, and skill of eastern Germans is believed to more than compensate for the lost cost advantage.

One German CEO explains, "It is as if you [Americans] could send your Mexicans home and replace them with well-educated, hardworking, highly skilled New Englanders whose native language was English" (Burstein, 1991). The work force in the German factories will begin to mirror the Japanese worker more than the American worker. The major problem remaining for the Germans is the high cost of the labor force—now the best paid in the world.

A key point in understanding the future of Europe and Germany is the view of eastern Germany as the gateway to the rest of Eastern Europe. Western Germany has already developed strong business relationships with eastern Germany limiting the entry of other countries. U.S. firms might be wise to form alliances with western German firms as they enter eastern Germany if they desire to be aggressive leaders into the rest of Eastern Europe. If you are giving thought to beginning a European subsidiary or expansion, you may want to consider Berlin or Dresden as the best place to be in the center of the New Europe.

Adopting the U.S. retail strategy called "sales"

But not all is rainbows and smiles in unified Germany. One challenge many firms are facing is teaching the eastern German workers the western German—or capitalistic—work ethic and performance standards. Executing those standards will be even more challenging.

The cost of reunification has taken its toll, resulting in high unemployment rates and slow economic times. In a country that historically has had retail sales only twice per year, it is now common to see sales signs in store windows year-round. Retailers simply say that sales are down. They need to attract consumers into the stores and move inventory. Many German consumers are now adopting the American buying habit of not wanting to buy something unless they are getting a deal.

The next ten years should be viewed as an investment and rebuilding period for Germany. Although some individuals will not be eager to sacrifice today in order to prosper tomorrow, nationalism likely will help ensure success. In the long run Germans will recognize that culture and language form a bond among people that not even walls can destroy. Although variations of culture and language may arise, the foundation built by ancestors—and cultural cornerstones such as Hegel, Goethe, Schiller, and Luther—will stand the test of time and the dictation of communism.

## *The Designated European Melting Pot*

As the two Germanies united, so did their demographic patterns. The birth rates in both countries continue to fall below replacement levels, signifying a decline in population in the united Germany. However, migration will play an important role in population growth in the next decade for both the western and eastern "territories." The year 1989 brought with it an immigration level of 845,000 people, 250,000 more than the official U.S. immigration numbers that same year. While residents of the former East and West Germanies share many similarities in values, they differ in marriage and family patterns. Those differences will have a significant impact on birth rates, which ultimately determine population trends.

Perhaps the most significant trend to affect the future of Germany is the influx of asylum seekers. We read about refugees in the papers and hear about them on national newscasts. But it is difficult to understand and comprehend the real effects on the entire nation until you discuss the topic with German citizens. Many feel reluctant to talk with outsiders for fear of being criticized for what we may feel to be cold reactions.

The United States was a party to enacting a German constitution that included the most liberal laws in the world for granting political asylum. The laws as written in the late 1940s recognized Germany's responsibility to be especially sensitive to those individuals facing severe persecution because of their resistance to oppressive political regimes. Germany needed to pay for its past sins, and it was forced to take in the downtrodden from the rest of the world, which might have seemed reasonable to most people at the time.

As so many times happens with something good, the system of welcoming the oppressed became a system of abuse. Germany had to guarantee a good life for anyone who claimed political asylum. The good life included free education, free health care, good housing, and a comfortable stipend—all without the requirement of working to pay for them.

Millions of migrants poured in from all over the world. People in Bangkok and poor countries all over the world tore up the passports of their children, made them swear not to tell their name or origin, and put them on planes to Frankfurt. The Germans were required by their constitution to take care of the millions of people who walked, drove, and flew from every poor country in the world. The problem of immigrants seeking asylum exists in the Netherlands, France, and other European countries but is most pronounced in Germany because it grants the most generous financial assistance.

Not only did the immigrants bring their hunger, illiteracy, and homelessness, they often brought their own values. The cost to taxpayers of feeding, housing, and medicating the hordes of people soon became oppressive in the minds of German taxpayers. Even more distressing was the fact that many immigrants did not believe in keeping homes fastidious as did the Germans, nor did they always place the same high value on education, science, family, and the church.

I have walked through the many government housing projects provided for immigrants and have seen something unheard of and unacceptable to most Germans: dirt, graffiti, and social disorganization. It was one thing to see the skinheads and neo-Nazis protest against the intruders, but when the government proposed that the elderly might have to be taxed on their beloved *Pension*, the support broadened for immigration control and those who protested against the *Ausländer*.

On a Ted Koppel "Nightline" program, the German minister of economics explained that Americans do not seem to understand the difference between citizenship and one's culture. "A person might be admitted as a citizen of Germany," the minister explained, "but that does not make that person German." Germans take very seriously the question of what it means to be German. I wonder why we seem to care so little about what it means to be American.

If you want to understand how to be successful in dealing with German business firms, it is very important to understand the German culture. If you want to understand why Germans have created higher wages per person than Americans and about half the work week of the Japanese, you must first of all understand the German culture. And when you do, you also understand why Germans are so concerned about the problem of asylum seekers and other immigrants who are believed to dissipate German values.

You can also understand why Germany is reevaluating the constitutional provisions for such immigration, learning perhaps from the successes of Switzerland and Singapore in how to maintain the culture of a country. Germany recently toughened its laws to make it more difficult for those seeking asylum to enter the country without showing passports at the airport. While in the past they were automatically given financial assistance, they are now sent back to their original ports of entry or home. The "seekers" protested!

## Name That Capitalism

The replacement for communism in Europe, the former U.S.S.R., and other portions of the globe is not simply capitalism. At least three viable contenders are competing for the title. A new war has begun among them. In the Battle of Capitalisms, the forms are as disparate as the American and the Japanese varieties. The new contender, however, is the German form.

German corporations are the foundation of the German economic system and provide role models for firms serious about prospering as global entities. Even smaller companies with no current interest or illusions about being global competitors need to study seriously the methods of German firms in order to compete effectively with companies that have global perspectives. Some of the lessons of German management can be applied effectively to firms that may never sell in other countries. The lessons of German firms are universal.

The German form of capitalism has produced results that are similar to the successes of the Japanese and American systems. All three countries have per capita income among the highest in the world, but they achieve it in different ways. The methods produce effects on quality of life that may appear subtle but in fact are profoundly different. Many observers of Japanese corporate life believe it is facing major challenges in the future as young workers seek more individualistic lifestyles, more emphasis on consumer goods rather than investment in industrial goods for export, expanded opportunities for women, and a better balance between work and family life.

German corporations have produced similar economic results but with different methods, strategies, and effects on employee lifestyles. Americans may have been reluctant to express much admiration for our former enemies, but it is time for a closer look at the reasons for the competitive successes of German corporations.

## *Fruits of Less Labor*

A closer look at Germany reveals a standard of living that is among the highest in the world and a quality of life for the masses of workers that would be the envy of most of the elite in the world. Leisure is one of the most desired goals of American workers and managers, but Germans already have leisure time with a standard work week of 37½ hours (don't bother calling German firms on Friday afternoon!). Vacations are mandated by law to be four weeks but are commonly six to eight weeks. Additionally, there are as many as nineteen paid holidays. Yet, with all that "nonproductive" time, German corporations have increased productivity faster in recent years than either Japanese or American corporations.

How long can this go on? The answer is we're not sure. As environments change, Germany might have to increase its productivity by increasing the number of part-time employees it hires. While more people would be employed, each would work less. Or Germany might have to demand that its workers work longer hours and more days per week. Or perhaps Germany will be able to maintain its phenomenon indefinitely.

In addition to high amounts of leisure coupled with high productivity and high income, the Germans have excellent food, excellent cars, excellent highways, excellent homes, excellent cities ringed by excellent forests, and excellent beer! They even serve it cold now. Leisure products from spas to boats are booming. And they seem to have enough time to learn to play tennis very well, as results at Wimbledon have vividly revealed!

Family life and cultural stability are under stress throughout the world with Germany as no exception. Because Germans tend to have more time to spend with their families and the money to support family activities, stability in values and family life should be expected. Maybe that is why the German government has recently extended maternity leave from 1½ years to 3 years, to be split as desired between the father and the mother. While the parent receives monetary compensation for only a portion of the time, his or her position is held for the entire three-year period. Some legislators have taken notice of this and are examining the American family leave situation. Which American firms will be the first to implement similar programs on their own?

Other employer benefits that may not be familiar to American readers include such staples as $360 a month each family receives during the first half-year of a child's life. Daimler-Benz for years has given $130 in cash for a child's birth and first communion and confirmation clothes. That was recently changed due to the competitive problem created by such generous benefits. Daimler-Benz even cut the Christmas bonus each worker gets from 80 percent of his or her monthly salary to the 60 percent that is required by law! Additional cuts in benefits provided by businesses and government are also being contemplated.

## *Gesundheit!*

The next time you want to wish someone who sneezes good health, you might try saying "*Gesundheit.*" Although you might end up as messy as the person who just sneezed, he or she will thank you just the same. *Gesundheit* is a word that is universally recognized to mean health. And you are more likely to get good health and good health care in Germany than in the United States or many other countries.

The German health care system is a combination of private and publicly funded programs—"Sickness Funds"—regarded by many observers to be the best in the world at providing quality care available to everyone. The Germans have more doctors per capita than Americans, are sick less often than most of their American or Japanese counterparts, and spend only 8 to 9 percent of gross domestic product to achieve such results compared to American expenditures of more than 14 percent.

In a recent trip to Germany, we found the greatest consumer complaint with the German health care system is that it did not pay for taxi fares to see a doctor! Think of the competitive disadvantage American firms face when they have to support a health care system at 14 percent and rising rapidly when firms in Germany pay only 8 percent with raises of less than 1 percent a year. Japanese firms pay even less, at only a little over 6 percent, with results superior to that of the American system. In fact the German infant mortality rate is much lower than our own in spite of the fact that (or maybe because) the majority of deliveries are assisted by midwives, rather than physicians.

One of the unique things about the system is that the Germans have a health care program rather than just a sickness care program. For example, if a person goes to the dentist once a year, insurance will pay 40 percent of the cost. But if a person has a checkup twice a year, it pays 80 percent of the cost. The rationale is that the person who visits the dentist twice a year, in the long run, will have lower dentist bills because of early diagnosis of problems such as cavities and gum disease.

Germans also go to the spa—oftentimes located in beautiful Bavarian towns—for a few weeks of rest and relaxation every three years. The corporate executives I've spoken to feel that preventive measures such as these make for healthier and happier employees, which in the long run adds to productivity.

Germans' focus on health has always been strong, even in somewhat controversial areas such as homeopathy. My wife's grandmother never came to America without a suitcase full of herbal remedies, including *Arnica, Spiritus,* and a variety of herb teas. She would be pleased to know that now some of those items are available in health stores located off the beaten track in some large cities. Traditional thinking might cause us to dismiss alternative medicines and treatments such as the spa experiences loaded with homeopathic treatments. But in Germany, such trips and other alternatives are funded by the German health care system and often prescribed and respected by doctors.

The German health care system encourages doctors to explore alternatives to healing patients. They do not take the position that if you have a problem, they can cut it out and make it better. Patients are given more options for the treatment of their illnesses, and often patient and doctor choose not to prolong the dying process as is common in the United States.

## Would You Like Mustard with Your Plate?

Living through the changes in our community's trash collection processes this past year has been enlightening. The system is simple—we all pay a measured amount depending on the amount of trash we create. We have watched with great interest as people find they only need to create about a third of the trash they used to dump. We have watched and cheered our town's and other communities' efforts to help in the new battle against trash.

While we may deserve kudos for our preliminary efforts, no country in the world expresses concern about the environment and controls pollution—and trash—at all levels as well as Germany. Years before most Americans even knew about the greenhouse effect, the problems with our landfills, and the benefits of recycling, Germany already had implemented programs addressing those issues.

In most residential areas of cities, you will find comprehensive recycling stations, marked "green bottles," "white bottles," "paper," and so forth. People collect their potato peelings and convert them to compost for their infinite number of gardens at the edge of every city. By law, manufacturers must provide recyclable shipping containers for packages sent to retail stores.

In the United States, Wal-Mart has taken the lead in creating a "green store" that serves as a prototype for many of the recycling processes that are expected to become the standard for manufacturing and retailing in the future. Many features that are new to Americans are standard practice in Europe. When German organizations implement innovations in recycling, they gain a competitive edge in responding to changes in consumer needs and expectations in terms of pollution control and packaging.

Riding on the train along the Rhine River, I ordered a German sausage with, of course, good German sauerkraut. It was almost as good as the sausage sold by Bob Evans. I was told by another passenger that the cardboard plates on which the sausages had been served created unwanted trash. So the Germans, with stereotypical practicality, solved the problem by creating an edible plate, something like a rice cake. I was told that after eating my sausage, I should also eat my plate. I did; it could have used a little mustard.

Evidence of Germany's commitment to recycling can be seen on many street corners

## *Trains to Nowhere*

German corporations are among some of the most profitable in the world. Corporations and government are both leveraged financially but both are conservative and avoid the excesses found in many countries, including the United States. Labor unions are ubiquitous but not uncooperative. They push for higher and higher standards of living for workers but work with management to achieve such standards through improvements in productivity. Usually, the unions are represented with members on the company's board of directors.

In Germany government generally facilitates the roles of both business and unions to achieve common goals. Tragically, our government takes the position—often reinforced in the media—that business is bad and needs to be regulated rather than supported.

Business does not seem to be perceived in Washington, as it is in Bonn, as the key to quality of life for everyone.

Breakdowns in the business-government-union alliance do occur. We arrived in Germany following strikes by the German railway workers. Germany had been faced with decision between giving raises to workers or continuing support for its new citizens, those from former East Germany and those seeking asylum from a variety of countries. The workers had foregone wage increases for several years but felt some reward was due. Because of the many hands pulling at Germany's pocketbook, management and government did not give in to the demands of the workers. A strike was inevitable.

Germany's trains did not run—a catastrophe to a nation that relies on mass transit and also prides itself on how well and efficiently it runs. Many Germans understood the workers' desire for wage increases; they indicated it was not always easy to give to and support others. The strike did not last long. In less than two weeks the trains were running again—on time.

The key to settlement was compromise. The workers did not get all the benefits they felt they were due, yet the government had to give in to some of their demands. Fair representation at all times, not just in times of trouble, helps keep the workers satisfied. But if an impasse is reached and strikes are necessary, the German system has a strong foundation for solving problems fairly quickly and smoothly.

In the United States, the union movement is based on the confrontation model, derived from the British model. The confrontation model conceptually is derived from the social idealism of Sidney and Beatrice Webb, whereas labor relations in other European countries are based more on the cooperation and social welfare model. Unions have declined from 35 percent of the labor force in the 1950s to less than 15 percent in recent years.

Some people say unions are no longer needed. That may be true if built on the British system but not necessarily true if they are built on the German system. German and British unions produce as different results as do union and nonunion work environments. It seems to me that unions in America would have a much better future if business and union theories were based on the premise of productivity and compromise rather than conflict and confrontation.

## *German Management 101*

German firms are able to offer their employees shorter work weeks, longer vacation periods, and higher labor wage rates than U.S. firms; yet the productivity of German firms is extremely high—often exceeding that of U.S. firms. What are some of the specific structures or processes that American firms can learn from the German model of management? In lectures and seminars I try to analyze them in more detail, but briefly they are the following:

*1. Small and midsize firms that concentrate on a market niche.* Chemical firms that made catalytic chemicals rather than commodities are examples, as are firms that concentrate on auto components rather than comprehensive manufacturing. The *Harvard Business Review* carried an article in 1992 documenting German niche firms, many of which have more than 50 percent market share worldwide. Often they have two or three times the market share of their nearest global competitor.

Dominance is created by relentless pursuit of a very specific market segment or niche, wherever in the world that segment may be found. Paints, thermostats, and other electric controls, automotive and other transport components, chemicals and other industrial products, are common examples of market dominance of a market niche on a global basis. For consumer products, such as apparel, Boss and Eskada provide excellent examples of success in a very specific niche (affluent men's or affluent women's clothing) in many countries of the world.

The German principle of niching or segmenting may be just the item you need for success in your company. IBM has now adopted that philosophy and is being broken up to thirteen medium-sized firms to try to solve some of the problems of the massive megacorporations that increasingly are dinosaurs. In Ohio, firms such as Symix (computer software), Cardinal Industries (wholesaler for independent grocery stores), and North American Life Insurance (pre-need funeral insurance) provide examples of how effectively the process of segmentation can work and how much money can be made by sticking to your niche. This principle can work even in multibillion dollar corporations such as 3M, which has thousands of products dominating little niches ranging from Buf-Pufs and Post-it notes to ceramic tiles for space vehicles.

*2. Research orientation.* In German factories, the plant manager often spends two hours a day reading academic research reports, indicates MIT professor Lester Thurow in some of his discussions of the reasons for German business success. "The devil is in the details," is a proverb well known to German engineering students. That philosophy so pervades the education of engineering and operations personnel that it leads to the development of a detailed orientation to production not readily duplicated in other countries.

The key, however, is more of a concentration on process rather than new products. Firms such as ABB Process Engineering, a European firm with important U.S. divisions, have created whole businesses based on process research.

One of the keys to American prosperity in the past and most certainly in the future is a similar emphasis on research and development in the applications or process area. The dilemma facing the United States, however, is that most of our major government-originated funds for research and development centered on military applications. Usually, the funds generated excellent results. We face major cutbacks in R & D expenditures in defense but have not created a funding mechanism, an institutional framework, or any clear idea of what the government's role should be, if any, in the future stimulation of a research and development culture in America.

In the past, when the government spent money on research

and development, everyone knew what we were trying to accomplish: Beat the Commies. Now most Americans and government leaders do not know who the enemy is or even if we have one, let alone how we should allocate research and development funds to fight whatever "war" we might be in and with what "weapons."

This dilemma does not mean that the typical business has to wait to develop a research culture. The best business firms, small or large, are always reading academic and trade journals, thinking about applications of many technologies, hiring managers and operatives who appreciate research and can understand it, allocate adequate funds for research, and inculcate a research orientation throughout the organization. It comes naturally for most German firms because it is part of the culture. Most Americans may need to work at developing the same spirit that supports a strong research orientation.

*3. Apprentice system.* One of the reasons German productivity is so high is because of the quality of workers produced by the apprentice system in Germany and other European countries. Workers are both more skilled and more educated than those produced by either American universities or our limited commitment to what we usually call vocational education. Les Wexner, chief executive officer of the Limited, recently made huge financial commitments to improving education. I believe we will never have a quality education system in the United States until business takes much more responsibility (probably more than government) for what is taught and how our students are prepared for their careers.

American businesses must realize that they are only fooling themselves if they expect American public schools to produce people who can compete in a global economy. A few entrepreneurs, such as those at Whittle Communications, are now proposing that private, for-profit schools will take their place beside the traditional public and private schools. A voucher system that would allow subsidies for students to be educated at such schools or any that are better than the existing ones would probably revitalize the decaying American educational system. Competent workers in the future may not come from American schools, however, until business leaders take a much different role—similar to the German apprentice system—in guiding the nature of the educational process.

4. *Better middle management.* If workers are better trained and more empowered, the need for middle managers is reduced. In the United States we have legions of middle managers who believe the key to improved income is a promotion or changing employers. In Germany, with fewer opportunities for promotion or changing employers, middle managers see the key to a better life as improving productivity in their present position. American firms can be dramatically improved when middle managers are instilled with a relentless desire to improve productivity in their present positions rather than depend on promotions for salary increases or improvements in working conditions.

In short, Americans are expressing concern about their own quality of life in dimensions as diverse as family life, job security, health care, food and homes for the poor, and the environment. The Germans have built such a good lifestyle that their costs may have risen too high, and some benefits will probably be reduced. But the fact remains that most Americans could trade places with Germans and find satisfaction on any of the key dimensions of quality of life.

As a way to manage corporations or a society, the Germans are establishing a new model for market economies. But we cannot disregard the problems with the German system, such as its general weakness in marketing when compared to its production and operations skills. There are negative as well as other positive attributes in the culture from which we could learn if we used more space for more details.

But the reality is this: Germany's form of capitalism is one that is based on principles and practices that produce highly efficient businesses capable of competing successfully in the global marketplace. Firms that seek success in the future can learn many lessons from Germany.

That's the way I see it, teetering on the edge of the wall.

# 5

# GOING DUTCH

## *A Date with Profitability*

**Think back to your school days:** Did you consider history to be one of the most fascinating topics to study or one of the most boring? Especially for those of you who fall into the second category, you might be surprised that some of the best ideas on how to be competitive globally are found in museums and history books. It's true, especially if those museums and history books are in the Netherlands.

In both historical Holland and modern-day Netherlands, you will find pervasive secrets of why some firms are consistently profitable year after year. These essential truths could be observed in the beginning of Dutch history—about a millennium ago.

## *Amstel: The River, not the Beer*

For our purposes Dutch history began with the Amstel River, which flowed unfettered from Europe to the Atlantic. To control flooding, the Dutch dammed the Amstel River. The result was a vibrant city, logically named Amsterdam.

The Amstel Dam created a problem for the many boats using the river for commerce. The Dutch could have ignored the concerns of its neighboring trading partners, but wisely they didn't. The Dutch did not want trouble and they did want something more. Had the Dutch taken the "It's not our problem" approach, others, such as the powerful Germans, might have destroyed the dam as well as the Dutch.

Instead, the industrious Dutch proposed a solution. They would provide the service of taking boats out of the river and carrying them around the dam. Furthermore, the proposed fee was so modest and the service so good, that the boat owners agreed to the Dutch service fee. Had the Dutch tried to take advantage of their monopoly power as so many firms in the United States appear to think they can do today, they probably would neither have prospered nor survived.

But the Dutch did survive and prosper, and so do firms that are built on the same principle. Provide a needed service. Do it well. Charge reasonable prices. Firms that follow that principle today are not very glamorous and may not always produce high margins. But they prosper in the long run and create fortunes for their owners.

## *Lessons from the Masters at the Rijksmuseum*

The Dutch pioneered the principle of global trade with good products and good service and tailoring their own ways to the culture of the country they were in, wherever in the world they might be. They did it so well that they dominated much of the world's trade for centuries with a tiny resource base and without much military power. You can verify the success of this principle by visiting, as I did in travels to the Netherlands, the museums of Amsterdam. Visit the Rijksmuseum and you can view with wonder the works of the great Dutch masters.

Amsterdam's museums differ from those of the rest of Europe in one important way. When you visit museums in the rest of Europe, the walls are dominated by massive paintings that take up much of the wall on which they're hanging. In Amsterdam museums, walls mostly contain small paintings.

Why are the Dutch masterpieces often small? Because they were originally commissioned by business families for their homes. The nation's money was concentrated among the Dutch business people. They were the people who could afford to have art created for them. They did not live in castles; instead they lived in modest, but comfortable, homes. The wall space was small and could house only small masterpieces. The paintings in the rest of the European museums are very large because only kings and the Church could afford them.

## *Make a Little on a Lot*

The key to early Dutch prosperity was conservatively managed, customer-oriented, fairly priced, globally skilled firms. The same holds true today for both the Netherlands and other countries or corporations that desire long-term prosperity and high shareholder value. The early Dutch traders were successful throughout the world because they believed success in the long run occurs when you make a little on a lot.

Do Dutch principles still work? Observe firms such as KLM (which handles distribution of so many U.S. magazines that it is the envy of most U.S. airlines), Unilever, and Shell to mention just a few. Or look at Philips, the Dutch firm that invented compact discs and is now extending this technology to CD-I (Compact Disc Interactive). How is it that so many massive firms are based in such a tiny country?

Or consider the fact that until recently, the Dutch owned more of America than any other country except the United Kingdom. Dutch investment policy has served the country ever since they traded a few trinkets for an island they called New Amsterdam—and which today is worth a few billion as Manhattan!

Would it surprise you also to learn that tiny Netherlands exports more value in agricultural products than Canada? Marketing people call it adding value to basic commodities. Most people just call it tulip bulbs.

## *The Dutch Live in Michigan*

It is not always high-tech, high-priced, glamorous firms that create lasting value. If you go to a Dutch-dominated culture such as Grand Rapids, Michigan, you still see the same principles in highly successful, privately owned Meijer's Thrifty Acres—known throughout the Midwest simply as Meijer, one of the few retailers to sell groceries, clothing, and hard goods successfully under one roof. In Grand Rapids, you also find other reflections of the Dutch culture in firms such as vacuum manufacturer Bissell and the nation's largest office furniture supplier, Steelcase Furniture. And of course, the Amway Corporation is based in Grand Rapids, spreading its success throughout the world through a philosophy of hard work.

## *Dutch Lessons: How to Find Value in the Stock Market*

Probably the most important lesson we can learn from understanding Dutch business principles is how to apply them to firms today. In many ways, the Dutch principles—good service and low prices—are the hallmark of America's most successful retailer, Wal-Mart. Many people regard Wal-Mart's success as a tribute to low prices, and that is certainly true. Less understood, but more important in my opinion, is Wal-Mart's emphasis on friendly, customer-oriented service. If you understand that principle and understand which firms have it, you are well on your way to being a Peter Lynch-style investor in the stock market. If you applied it to Wal-Mart over the long haul, you were richly rewarded.

An application of the Dutch approach to business can be observed in firms such as Consolidated Stores, the largest "close out, buy-out" merchant in the United States. Headed by CEO Bill Kelley, the firm has built an impressive record of growth and profits with its Odd Lots and All For One stores that caused the stock to quadruple in value in the early 1990s. Go into one of its All For One stores and you will not find much glamour—just good service, pleasant (not ostentatious) surroundings and very low prices. In fact, every price is one dollar. The ancient Dutch burghers surely would have approved!

## *Keeping Up with the Joneses*

As you walk around Amsterdam or the wonderful villages in the country, you will be impressed with how neat and clean but unpretentious the homes are. Comfortable but practical. I was similarly impressed when I walked around the headquarters of Edward D. Jones, America's largest stock brokerage firm with more than 2,200 offices. Clean and comfortable but inexpensive is the best way to describe the Jones headquarters as well as those of many of the best-managed firms.

That is why you will find the headquarters of some of the best-managed firms in places such as Bentonville, Arkansas, and St. Louis, Missouri. Merrill Lynch reportedly pays more per square foot to rent its fancy Wall Street offices than Edward D. Jones paid to buy its headquarters in St. Louis. To me, keeping up with the Joneses should be measured by the cost per square foot, not by ostentation.

The principles worked when the Dutch dammed the Amstel River. They work just as well one thousand years later.

## *Don't Skip Schiphol!*

What else can you learn by visiting the Netherlands? Much, just by observing Amsterdam's Schiphol Airport, possibly the most efficient airport in Europe. As a result, the air fare to Amsterdam for a business class round-trip ticket from major cities in the United States is often about a thousand dollars less than to London or Paris. Wise Europeans take a train to Amsterdam and depart from Schiphol instead of from Heathrow or DeGaulle. The next time you go to Europe, you may want to do the same.

If your schedule permits, fly to Amsterdam and either pocket the savings for your firm or use them for a few extra days in the European city of your choice. If you did not already know about this, you have just saved one thousand dollars by reading this book. It is just one more example of what I mean by increasing profitability, Dutch style!

You will also find many logistics-oriented firms around Schiphol. A recent European study by A. T. Kearny shows that firms can cut their transportation costs from 14 percent to 6 percent by having a leadership approach to logistics management. You'll find more than their share of logistics leadership firms based in the Netherlands.

## *Can Schiphol Be Shipped to U.S. Airports?*

What else will you find at Schiphol airport? Not only some of the most interesting shops in airports but ones that charge reasonable prices. This, I think you will agree, is a novel idea for most airports.

The Dutch approach to airports is beginning to be applied in the United States, however. It started when Minneapolis installed the golden arches of McDonald's inside the airport. I attended a conference several years ago where airport managers were asked the question, Why can't U.S. airports be like Schiphol? The answer is, they can be.

The best example of an entire airport built more along the

Schiphol principle is the new Pittsburgh International Airport with successful retailers and interesting shops such as the Body Shop and TGI Friday's. Prices, signs proclaim throughout the airport, are no higher than in the surrounding trade area.

The Schiphol principle of airports having top-notch shops with normal prices can also be seen in Columbus. Port Columbus is home to J. D. Barrett, possibly the best little apparel shop in any U.S. airport. In Port Columbus, you will also find Nutcracker's Suite, which sells fantastic handmade chocolates fresh daily, an airport rarity. Chocolate-covered raspberries and strawberries are among the favorites of travelers. The name of the shop is derived from the fact that it also sells handmade nutcrackers imported from Europe. I've been told that airline personnel from all over the nation seek out the good selection of reasonably priced nutcrackers at Port Columbus.

I can verify the quality of the chocolates; my wife and I find them a tempting alternative to food that awaits us on most airlines!

Both of the stores are small, privately owned firms. It should be encouraging to many readers that even small businesses can apply the Dutch principles of good products and services at fair prices built on a transportation-oriented economy. I know both of the business-owners. They are women who have taken their ideas to the airport and, with a lot of care and hard work, turned them into successful businesses.

But you don't need to have a store present in the airport to apply the concept of attracting a transportation-oriented customer base. Just ask Marvin Williams. His six- to eight-page sections advertising scan-card systems and motivational posters are found in airline magazines around the globe attracting a large, captive audience every day. All of the advertising is prepared in his own low-cost computer operation, a good application of the Dutch principles to the creation of low-cost, but effective, advertising. In fact, he has even tied into the museum concept of Holland I discussed in the beginning of this chapter. The name of the company, of course, is the Executive Gallery.

If you get some fresh-baked cookies on a Delta flight or some excellent cookies on USAir or other airlines, there is a good chance they were prepared by Cheryl and Co., also started near the Columbus airport. Cheryl Krueger started making cookies in her home at Christmas and expanded into a number of retail shops. Now the growth part of her business is with millions of dollars of sales to airlines and other food operations. Good products, fair prices, and constant attention to the changing nature of transportation and economic or cultural conditions. The principles worked for the Dutch. They are working for many entrepreneurs today.

## *The Resort for Green Consumers*

If you are looking for a back-to-nature approach to vacations and want to observe and meet European families, Center Parcs might be the solution. My wife, friends, and I stayed at a Center Parcs resort on one of our trips. It is a unique value- and environmentally oriented destination resort based in the Netherlands but with locations in several European countries. It is affordable fun for the family. Its high occupancy rate proves it is a rival in its own way to Disney World. The emphasis, however, is on the environment. Families go to the parks to learn about and respect plants and animals in their natural settings, as well as to have a lot of fun in the water and other sports centers enclosed under a huge bubble environment that also houses restaurants and retail shops.

With environmental concerns so close to the hearts of European families, the parks have been a great success. Reportedly, Center Parcs may soon come to the United States, bringing this unique Dutch concept to increasingly green consumers.

As you travel around the Netherlands, I hope you will do it the way the Dutch do—walk or ride bicycles. Bicycles certainly are the greenest of vehicles, and you will find them everywhere, even in winter. In the winter, however, you may also see a lot of people skating on frozen canals. Besides saving gas, saving money, and sav-

Center Parcs: A vacation concept based on returning to nature

ing air pollution, the use of bicycles by people of all ages saves one other thing: lives. The good health of the Dutch, in the face of the rich pastries and cheese-laden food they make so well, has to be attributed largely to the amount of exercise people get when they walk and ride bicycles at all ages.

## *Key to Prosperity: Poor Natural Resources?*

If you travel around the world, you can easily observe that the people who have the most natural resources are usually the poorest. The people who are born in countries with almost nothing often end up with the most prosperity.

This is certainly true in the Netherlands. The Dutch had very little land so they created more of it from the ocean. They have very small space for farming but they create huge exports from tulips, cheese, and other value-laden products. They have little natural scenery to attract tourists, so they created the world's most efficient airport to attract travel and distribution.

England and France are probably better known as European business locations, so the Dutch have created incentives and business facilitating services that make the Netherlands one of the most attractive locations for European subsidiaries of U.S. firms. Checkpoint is an example of a New Jersey-based international manufacturer of security systems for retailers. It recently changed its European operations from a U.K. distributor to a Dutch-based subsidiary and in the process acquired excellent Dutch technology and distribution knowledge.

The Netherlands had few minerals, so the Dutch created a trading and shipbuilding empire that even today spans the world from Djakarta to Cape Town to New York. They had floods, so they created a dam, and from that dam they created one of the most prosperous cities and countries in the world. The Dutch have certainly made a lot from a little.

A trip to the Netherlands will open the mind to history, art, knowledge, and business. But if you go to the Netherlands, you will see a lot more than museums, as fascinating as they are. Look closely at the principles on which this tiny country's amazing prosperity is built. They are the same principles that can produce prosperity for any company or person. Solve a problem, do it well, and price the product or service reasonably. The Dutch principle of make a little on a lot is not very glamorous. But the principle can create a fortune for the people who understand and apply it.

It was once said that unless we understand history, we are doomed to repeat it. It is my hope that we will learn from Dutch history and repeat it, indeed.

That's the way I see it . . . from the edge.

# 6

# POLAND

*Star in the East*

KRISTINA STEPHAN BLACKWELL

**Did you hear the Polish joke about** . . . ? If you bristle instead of laugh when you hear those words, there is good news. Those who are getting the last laugh are those who understand some of the business opportunities that are unfolding in this always changing, politically and geographically complex country.

But there is much more than economic development for me to consider when I think about Poland.

Kristina Stephan Blackwell, wife of Roger Blackwell, received undergraduate and M.B.A. degrees from The Ohio State University in logistics, marketing, and international business and has lived and worked in Europe. Tina and Roger are coauthors of *Contemporary Cases in Consumer Behavior*, a textbook that contains examples of the strategies and marketing programs of domestic and global companies.

# POLAND
*Star in the East*

## Somewhere in Time

Traveling much of the world before the age of thirty has given me a variety of perspectives on life. Those perspectives include not only the best ways to conduct business but also the ways we should and do conduct ourselves. I have always tried to learn lessons from people of other countries. That process is the basic theme of this book. But there are times when I have felt overwhelmed. My trip to Poland was one of those times.

Perhaps the awe associated with Poland was because it was my first encounter with a former Communist country. Or perhaps it was because of my inability to communicate with many of the people. But most likely it was because I was there to learn not only about other people, but also about myself.

You often hear or read about people traveling to uncover their roots buried deeply beneath years of lost information and forgotten family ties. But I was fortunate to have my father as my own personal guide in Poland. As it turned out, he was really on the same sentimental journey that I was.

My father was born in the city of Lodz, which housed a large ethnically German population. For many years he wondered what had happened to his birthplace, the school he attended, and the home in which he spent his first thirteen years. His family had been forced to flee during World War II, salvaging only the clothing they could carry and the memories in their hearts.

For my father, that meant carrying with him years of unresolved issues and many unanswered questions. For me it meant having an incomplete picture of my heritage and background. When the doors to Poland were opened and the opportunity arose, my father and I went to learn about our pasts and the country's future.

## The Protective Curtain

Returning to your birthplace after nearly half a century is probably never easy. The return is made more difficult when that country has

66

been inaccessible to most people for many years. That is what happened to Poland because of what was once called the Iron Curtain.

Many people think the curtain changed the way Eastern Europe functioned and fared in the postwar era. In reality, it did exactly the opposite. The Iron Curtain acted as a shield behind which Poland and the other Eastern European countries were forced to adopt the ways of a Communist regime. In fact, those countries were caught in a time capsule in which they continued to operate in times long gone. It was the rest of the world that changed, adapted, and forged ahead. The Iron Curtain prevented Poland from experiencing those changes.

As I prepared to enter Poland, the question in my mind was, How will Poland and the other Eastern European countries fare in the global competition faced by market economies? How well will the Polish people do in their quest for the riches of capitalism?

The answers to these questions vary greatly among each of the former Communist nations. The answer in Poland and in other Eastern European countries seems to depend on the view of change held by the citizens of each country. The answers also depend on the long-term vision shared by each nation's citizens and on how well they are prepared for the future.

A country's commitment to all of those values is only as strong as the feelings of the country's individuals. In the weeks we spent visiting Poland, we learned about and came to understand the realistic outlook on the future of the average Polish citizen.

## Coffee, Tea, or Pierogi?

We arrived in Warsaw on Lufthansa. In retrospect, we should have taken Poland's LOT airlines in order to experience firsthand one of Poland's business successes. Significant hurdles face many of the Eastern European carriers, but LOT seems to be making the changes needed to compete in the new western world.

LOT leaders have upgraded the fleet with numerous B-767s,

now that the company is not forced to buy Soviet planes. The airline has also increased its routes to other countries, including the United States. LOT still faces a major problem, however—the lack of currency. But it has solved the problem with as much ingenuity as possible by working with other airlines on cooperative routes to various U.S. destinations, until LOT can afford to add more planes to the fleet. It is interesting to note that regardless of country of origin, if a company or product is good and of high quality, it will survive in the competitive world economy—even if it is a former Communist venture.

## Color My World

A first impression, they say, is something that is difficult to change. We host many foreign visitors in our home, and we often ask them to summarize their findings about the United States in ten words or less. Phrases such as "A rainbow of color" or "Where are the cowboys and Indians?" would be the most common answers.

Probably the most frequently mentioned characteristic foreign travelers note about the United States is its size. They are amazed at the bigness of our country, homes, stores, and even portions of food we eat—and therefore the size of the average person as well. We forget how fortunate most of us are to have affordable and comfortable homes. We forget that most of the world does not shop in a retail center with Wal-Mart, K-Mart, Sears, Target, and Meijer just footsteps away from one another.

Another characteristic people often comment on is the ethnic diversity of our country. Having just watched a report on the national news about the problem of racially based violence that occurs in our nation daily, one of our visitors recently asked us if the flame under the melting pot had gone out. It was a question we did not know how to answer, but my initial reaction was to explain that the country was checking its pilot light.

While the image of the American cowboy and his struggle

with the Indians has not completely left the minds of many foreign travelers, it has faded somewhat in the last ten years. Yet people still ask us where they can find the typical American cowboy. It is then that we point to the billboards lining America's highways—or drive-by art museums—and introduce them to the most famous cowboy of all, the Marlboro Man.

If I had to summarize Poland, it would only take one word—gray. The weather is gray, the buildings are gray, the people are gray. At first glance the mood of the country might also seem gray. It is only once you get to know the people that you recognize a palette of bright colors hidden beneath Poland's gray exterior. Poland's colors can be called hope, optimism, and commitment. An artist might use blue, yellow, and purple on his canvas to describe what the country will look like when individuals' values collectively leap from behind the gray shadows of a Communist legacy.

## *Solidarity in Soft Times*

My first conversation in Poland was with our cab driver. If there is one thing I've learned over the years, it's that everyone can learn something from every cab driver. That is especially true in a foreign country. (The only places where this principle may not hold true are Washington, D.C., and New York City—but only because the taxi driver probably does not speak much English!)

It was from our taxi driver that I heard my first discussion about optimism for Poland's future. It was clear that the optimism was very much influenced by his personal hero, Lech Walesa. In a sense, it was similar to what I have heard from people quoting Martin Luther King, Jr. It was the kind of optimism that one sometimes hears from people who face great obstacles but who still have a dream for what might be and what they believe can be in the future.

The Solidarity movement came to official power in 1990, after many years of building support underground. With Solidarity came hope for Polish workers. The hope was based on European Community models. The plan, simply stated, was to jump the wall that had isolated Poland for nearly a half century and develop Poland into a modern European country. Although Poland has not been immune to the difficulties of changing political and economic structures, it has made significant progress toward that goal. Poland is on the road to establishing a viable market system.

Throughout Poland we heard people speak of the future, just as our cab driver did. They told us that they knew the future was uncertain. But the uncertainty was not about getting better or worse. The uncertainty was about the speed of change and the degree of improvement. Realistic people acknowledged that hard times were ahead. They were willing to face those hard times. But change as rapid and dramatic as in Poland can be troubling regardless of how optimistic people want to be. This can be seen in the recent Polish elections.

Our cab driver told us how pleased he was to see all of the foreign visitors, although it was hard for him to understand why we would ever want to leave the United States even for a vacation. For him and other workers, increased interest in his country from outsiders meant a greater possibility of foreign investment. Even though the unemployment rate has increased since the transition to a free market system, he explained to us that he saw foreign investment as a positive sign. He was able to see beyond the short-term problems and realize that with foreign investment would come stability, hard currency, and an increased standard of living.

Why are the Polish people willing to sacrifice to overcome tough times? The answer they gave me was always clear: they wanted better opportunities for their children.

Sacrificing in our own lifetime for the future of the next generation is something we all should understand better, and be selfless enough to do. Perhaps it is easier to sacrifice and be selfless when we feel life can only get better. The downside to such an investment is minimized in deprived countries and soft economic environments.

Perhaps the opposite is now true in the United States. More and more, we are told, people in the United States feel the future will be worse than the past. Today's youth are told in the media that they must be prepared for a lower standard of living than their parents have. In many ways, belief in the Eastern European nations parallels the early part of the last century in America. There will be rewards for those who work hard. The future will be better!

## The First Western Icon

Poland is a gray country. Nearly every block of every city and in every village, the visitor's eyes see little except gray, deteriorating buildings housing families, shops, and factories. There is one shining exception. Although new construction is beginning to be spotted in various places, the Warsaw Marriott was the first Western icon.

It is easy to spot the shiny, new Warsaw Marriott. The Marriott has been *the* hub of business as well as much political activity since it opened. The lobby was buzzing with different languages and the sounds of alliances being formed. Nearly every topic in business or politics could be overheard and in nearly every language of the world. It was the closest one could come to a real-world, modern version of the intergalactic bar in the movie *Star Wars*!

We observed another surprising fact in the Warsaw Marriott. In this Polish-American hotel, few Americans conducted business. There were many Germans, an abundance of Japanese businesspeople, and a sampling of many other industrial powers of the world. The lack of American businesspeople was noticeable. The few Americans who seemed to be there on business appeared to represent agricultural interests.

The $65 million hotel was a welcome sign of commitment and future investment in Poland. It is the perfect example of a global strategic alliance done well. In fact, it was the first joint venture under Polish law. Under the agreement and joint venture contract No. 001, Marriott owns 25 percent of the hotel, with Ilbau, an Austrian construction firm, owning 25 percent and LOT airlines owning 50 percent.

Even though the building and its amenities are impressive, the physical attributes are outshined by the level of service offered by enthusiastic Warsaw Marriott employees. The majority of the more than one thousand employees are native Poles with no hotel experience. Marriott executives felt that those with previous hotel and restaurant experience probably had the wrong type of experience. Although they did not have many of the skills needed to perform their hotel duties, they did possess the natural hospitality and verbal skills needed to make the Warsaw Marriott run as smoothly as (if not more smoothly than) its Western counterparts.

The hotel valets, bellboys, and waitpersons were more than willing to tell their guests how proud they were to work at the Marriott. One young man we talked to had joined the Marriott team and was working at the front desk. In almost perfect English he told us how he had left his job as a doctor to work for Marriott. At first glance, we might assume the career change occurred only because of the higher wages and perks, including two free meals per day, uniforms, shoes, and free language lessons offered by the hotel. But such an assumption would be wrong.

The real reason for working for a well-managed, western firm is opportunity to learn and the ability to embrace change. While many of us fear change, the brave and bright-eyed men and women we met in Poland seemed to face it head on with optimism. In Poland I saw many young people who were preparing any way they could for the changes to come.

## What's for Sale in Warsaw?

The answer to that question had changed dramatically in the last year. Poland had been a country where people had sufficient money to buy the products they needed and wanted, but nothing was available to buy. It has now become a country of abundant supply of products and consumers with little buying power. Simply stated, the answer to the question of what's for sale in Warsaw is everything!

Although consumers might not be able to afford many products—due in part to double-digit inflation—they are packing the stores. Consumers might not buy in high quantities, but they certainly are interested in buying. And retailers are more than willing to sell.

The buying process is different in Poland from the United States. Most of our merchandise is displayed in open aisles for us to handle, try on, and put in our shopping carts. To discourage theft, mostly of small items, small retailers usually place items behind counters and glass display cases. Can you imagine going to Kroger or Safeway and waiting for a salesperson to make your food selections for you?

This is true even when buying clothing items such as shoes. The open store displays used in most retailers such as Pic Way Shoe Marts, Hush Puppies, and Florsheim would be a luxury in most Polish retail stores. In fact Poland would be a great market for Checkpoint Systems. By placing antitheft tags on clothing and other products, retailers could take them from behind the counters and literally place their products in the hands of thousands of potential consumers.

An area that had not been developed well in Poland was merchandizing. Not only did the store window displays leave much to be desired, but so did the packages of many of the food items. While the packaging has improved in the last year, there are still many plain, brown cookie boxes to be found. In one of our visits to a small grocery store, Dole pineapple was selling like hotcakes. Not only was it a fairly new and tasty American treat, it was also packaged in the brightest, most colorful cans and labels we could find. There was a definite need for color in a world of gray weather, gray buildings, gray packages, and gray clothing.

Poland's capitalistic entrepreneurial crusade

## *Sam Walton Would Be Happy*

During our stay in Warsaw, I was amazed by the constant retail activity occurring everywhere. Perhaps the informal sector was even more busy than the formal sector of the economy. In fact one "company" we visited was located on one of Warsaw's busiest streets. The president took us on a tour of the store and showed us his product line—from auto parts to T-shirts. Although we weren't sold on any of the products, I believe it was the vice-president of marketing who convinced us that a pair of light blue cotton socks was a great buy. You see, the vice-president was a seven-year-old boy, his sales clincher was a set of huge, innocent brown eyes, and the store consisted of two blankets stretched out on a sidewalk of busy downtown Warsaw.

This was not the only store of its kind in Poland. In fact there were portions of the city in which it was difficult to walk because of the overabundance of Poland's new generation of entrepreneurs.

It would be an understatement to say the entrepreneurial spirit was everywhere present. But that would not be a surprise to those who look back at Poland's history.

Even after World War II, much of Poland's agricultural land was owned and operated by individual farmers, who in a sense were entrepreneurs in their own right. Some did work in co-ops to provide some of the country's staple items, but many farmers were able to work as agriculture entrepreneurs. This is still true today. More than 80 percent of all farmlands are organized as private farms, with the average size being only six hectares.

On our way to Lodz, Poland's second-largest city with nearly one million inhabitants, we were able to see some of those farms from our train window. The small farms were plowed with old equipment often seen in early twentieth-century museum exhibits. But for independently run small farms, with small operating budgets, the equipment, although not ideal, seemed to do an adequate job.

Poland's aspiring entrepreneurs have prepared themselves well for their role in their country's future. The Poles are among the best educated individuals in Europe. A free education is provided to all children to the age of sixteen. While many of the males complete more technical forms of education, the females tend to complete secondary school. The need to understand how to survive in a new market economy has sparked much interest in business courses. The education system has responded accordingly by offering more business courses at various education levels.

Perhaps one of the more practical ways Poland's new entrepreneurs have prepared themselves for the future is by learning other languages, primarily English. With much of the tourism being composed vastly of business travel, many potential customers for small operations are foreign businesspeople. Chances are, if the travelers cannot speak Polish, they can speak either German or English. So can the Poles. And most of them can usually speak an additional Slavic language—especially Russian—as well. I was impressed with the proficiency of the English language most people we spoke with during our shopping sprees possessed.

As the informal sector of retailers moves from the sidewalks of Warsaw to its retail stores, communication will become a vital business tool. Just ask US West. One of our country's most promising business leaders, Sol Trujillo, president of US West Direct, understands the vast opportunity for communication services in Poland. While other business leaders sometimes bemoan the problems of working in Eastern Europe, Trujillio has led his company, one of the most successful Yellow Pages companies in the United States, to be the same in Poland. In fact, the US West project in Poland is progressing so well that it is not only meeting profit targets but is running ahead of schedule.

Projects such as that are for U.S. firms that must seek new profit opportunities by competing in the global marketplace. Even more important, perhaps, is the contribution of such firms to the marketplace in the formerly Communist countries. While US West is profiting by selling Yellow Pages advertising, it is also providing a valuable service—educating small businesses of Poland about when and how to use advertising. The Yellow Pages salesperson is probably the best trained—and probably the most appropriate—source of information about advertising (and perhaps general business knowledge) that the many emerging small businesses are likely to be able to access.

# POLAND
*Star in the East*

## Times They Are Unchanged

Visiting Lodz was my most important reason to travel to Poland. This was the land of my father's boyhood, where I eagerly looked forward to seeing his—and in a fanciful, nostalgic sense, my—family home. I had heard my father and my grandmother speak of it with fond memories and with pride. But what would we find? Would the family home still be standing or would it have given way to a bulldozer?

We walked down the street and turned the corner. My father gave a sigh of relief. The house was still standing but now it was very deteriorated. The decay and disorder left distraught my father's ethnically German need for organization and cleanliness. In a testimony to the reality of the Communist regime, the house had been divided into nine apartments. Scenes from the movie *Dr. Zhivago* could not have described better the feelings when one who once owned a home sees it given over to the communal system for random allocation to families.

The school my father attended as a child had changed, yet stayed the same, since his boyhood. He remembered fondly his school friends and the games children play around the world even to this day. He also remembered school days filled with order, discipline, and uniforms. My father swears that the chairs and desks used by today's students were the same ones he had used fifty years ago. But the stone building suffered severely from graffiti warfare that no one had removed. It would be the first time I would see my father cry.

Nothing illustrates the plight of the various ethnic communities of Poland and most of Europe during the decades under Communist rule as well as the gray buildings. Very little was invested in infrastructure. Communistic philosophy dictates that capital is unimportant, unneeded, and even evil. The buildings of Poland demonstrate vividly the effects of that philosophy. Much of the city was unchanged for decades.

The most ironic aspect of the gray, deteriorating buildings is found among the structures that have been repaired and painted. What color did the Communists choose when they did put new paint on old buildings layer after layer? You guessed it. Gray! Maybe the Communists should have been called the Grays rather than the Reds.

To say that nothing has changed is not really accurate. In a sense, the city has changed dramatically because of its inability to maintain itself over the years. Lodz was once noted throughout Europe for its intricate, detailed building fronts and superior architecture. Now it has become a testament to the difficult times suffered behind the Iron Curtain. While Warsaw was beginning to get its face-lift, Lodz was struggling to remain presentable with yet another layer of makeup called gray paint.

## *The Grass Is Rarely Greener*

Perhaps one of the most disturbing occurrences in our society is how we, all of us included, take our standard of living for granted. We complain when we can't afford to buy the new sports car of our dreams. We curse the President and the horrible state of our economy when we can't buy the new house we feel we all deserve because we work forty hours a week. Our teenagers are outraged and think their parents are unfair when told they can't buy that $150 pair of sneakers or jeans.

None of us is immune to feeling we are at the receiving end of life's more painful kicks in the behind now and again. But it is the lifestyles and expectations of many of our young people that is discouraging and often infuriating. While more of our high school and college students are working to make a contribution to their pocketbooks, not many of them are managing their money well. One would think that their parents would teach them or force them to place a majority of their money into savings accounts to eventually be used for higher education or maybe a down payment on a house.

But many of them spend their money on fashion clothing and fairly expensive cars. Eventually, when school is over and they have to support themselves, they are not able to live in the same manner they were accustomed to while in mom and dad's cozy nest.

In the past, upon graduation from college and even high school, young people were able to find a job, get married, and buy a house. But things have changed. Young men and women are finding it more difficult to live the same type of secure lifestyle their parents were able to enjoy. They are having to settle for jobs for which they feel overqualified—even though this is often a case of ego rather than fact—and live in apartments that may have only one bedroom and may not face the swimming pool of their apartment complex.

While I may seem insensitive to the very real frustrations of many of our young—and more recently, older—population, it is to make a point. We are often not able to remember the things that we do have because we are always focused on the things we don't have. It is a weakness we all succumb to at times. But I lose some of my sympathy for those who always think of themselves as unfortunate when in reality they live better than a majority of the rest of the world. I wish I could take all the teenagers in this country to Lodz or other recovering cities around the world. Everyone's words of thanks around the Thanksgiving table would change drastically. While taking everyone to Lodz is an impossibility, perhaps my contribution to unknowingly fortunate teens can be my recollection of a modern-day struggle for survival.

## A Day in the Life

I was waiting in the lobby of the Grand Hotel for my father, who had left early Sunday morning to arrange for a taxi driver to spend the day with us. In his broken Polish and the driver's limited German, he was able to communicate to the driver where we wanted to go. Although all of the street names had been changed from the

German names my father remembered to Polish ones, eventually we found each destination on our day's itinerary.

We could not have asked for a better or more patient guide as we documented our trip with pictures and movies. He stood with us when we began attracting too much attention when filming my father's old home and school. He also told us when it was safe to photograph streets, buildings, and people. He expressed his concern with the rising crime rate occurring in Lodz. "Poverty brings out the devil in people" were words I remembered both in Lodz and at home.

By the end of the day, we had gained a new friend. He told us we must come to his home for coffee and cake. He had already instructed his wife to go to town and buy the best pastries she could find. Having company, especially foreign guests, was cause for celebration. While we knew how much it cost him to entertain us for the afternoon, we did not want to offend him by turning down his generous hospitality.

We arrived at the parking lot of his apartment building. It was a typical gray high-rise—old and neglected from the outside. But I quickly realized that the outside was a pleasant facade for what I found on the inside. We walked up five flights of stairs and entered a dark corridor that accessed eight apartments and one community bathroom. Our friend explained to us that, humble as it might be, he was lucky to have an apartment at all. He had waited for it for several years.

His apartment was at the end of the corridor. It seemed an eternity just to reach the door of a thousand locks. We were greeted by three eager hostesses: the driver's wife, mother, and daughter. The four of them shared the one-bedroom apartment, which would be considered very small on our bloated American scale. Although I could not speak with the little girl, she took my hand and showed me her room. It was a portion of the living room that had been sectioned off by a makeshift wall and decorated with newspaper and wrapping paper. She was proud to show me her doll and promptly put it in my arms to carry. I think sharing was a lesson she had mastered early by watching her parents.

We gathered at the small folding table that had been placed in the middle of the main room and set with the family's finest china. We ate, drank, and laughed together, momentarily forgetting our unpretentious surroundings.

The family explained to us that they had been placed on a waiting list to get a larger apartment, but they did not know how many years they would have to wait. At the time the average Polish worker made approximately $120 per month, which has since increased along with inflation rates. Our friend averaged $100 per month, but with his family's saving strategies, they were able to get by without too many problems.

I asked him why he thought Poland would fare better than other Eastern European countries in the change to a free market system. He seemed to attribute the hopeful prognosis to the dedication of the majority of people to the cause. Yet he did express some concerns about work habits. Workers would have to be educated and trained to survive in a workplace that expected them to work five days a week. Under previous Communist conditions, employees would often not show up to work for various reasons because they were guaranteed a job regardless of performance record. While that work ethic was now habit, the driver felt that if workers were allowed to benefit more based on good performance, the habit would not be hard to break.

My initial reaction was one of pity. I explained to him with much sincerity how I felt. But he quickly interjected. While times were difficult, he explained, they had turned the corner. He, of course, wanted more for his family but felt that earning an honest living, coupled with changes in the political system, would lead to better economic times.

He told us not to feel sorry for them because in many ways

they were very blessed. They had good health, shelter, food, family, and clothing. And he knew that one day his daughter would have opportunities that he had never had.

During our time with that remarkable family, we talked of the problems faced by many Polish people, especially those living in smaller cities. But most of our discussions did not focus on what the government was doing wrong or how the economy was suffering.

We discussed how individuals should take more active roles in deciding their own fates in a rapidly changing world. I was surprised by how the family refused to blame other people, countries, and governments for their economic predicament, something that is all too popular in many industrialized countries today. We also talked about hope, faith, and the future. Those are the things people in recovering countries should focus on if they are to survive their economic challenges with sanity intact. I also think that we would benefit from a similar outlook.

After our visit, it was time to return to the Grand Hotel. The day's fare was twenty dollars, for which we gladly gave our friend a thirty-dollar tip—almost one third of his monthly wage.

We parted that evening, all of us having gained varying perspectives on life. I often think of the taxi driver and his family. We did keep in contact for a while sending care packages of coffee, T-shirts, and other "luxury" items. But the packages never reached the family.

They have since moved, perhaps to the two-bedroom apartment they had been waiting for. I wonder how they are doing and if they'll remember us. I wish I could tell them how much they helped me understand their country and how they changed my life.

I learned a valuable lesson in that small apartment in Lodz. You see, when you are sitting on a putting green, while there might be some divots in sight, the grass is never greener on the other side. Now when I slip into that human weakness called self-pity, I feel the hard boots of my father and our Polish friends on my behind, and I quickly thank God for what I have.

Then I strategically plan how to attain the things I would like to accomplish. Ambition, when kept in perspective, is not a sin.

## *Reflections on the Future*

Reflecting on the time my father and I spent in Poland, and later with family in Germany, I think of the lessons learned from the people we met and experiences we shared. Personally, I understand better now when my father says the one prayer he has for me is that I never live through a war fought in my country. I understand better the complexities people feel when confronting cultural issues. I understand that it is our own responsibility to learn about the various parts of our backgrounds and integrate the best characteristics from each one to form our own special identities.

More importantly, I learned how to view change differently. Basic instinct and the law of inertia both dictate that change is an undesirable state. It is much easier to remain in situations that are familiar even though they might be detrimental in the long run. I don't know when I have seen a group of people as willing to go through painful changes for good in the long run.

Many Poles have found entrepreneurship to be the answer to getting through tough times. Others find work in more structured areas to be more secure. But Poland's spirit to succeed in the new free market economy is present everywhere and seems to be contagious.

That's the way I see it, with perhaps a little different perspective from my husband, . . . from the edge!

# 7

# HONG KONG

*On the Edge of the Orient*

**A city of a thousand smells.** That is one description of Hong Kong. Many of those mysterious odors of the Orient exude from shops selling exotic spices, perfumes, fortune cookies, and other treasures from the East. Other odors are not so nice. Fresh meat hanging in the one-hundred-degree sun of Hong Kong's side streets; geese, chickens, and other poultry hanging by their naked necks in unrefrigerated poultry stalls; cages of live frogs jumping to the top to become someone's dinner. Most dominant of all the odors is that of the omnipresent harbor, smelling of fish and floating garbage dumped by thousands of boat families.

## *The Most Exciting City in the World!*

The smells, along with the brightly colored lights that illuminate shops throughout the night are all a part of what makes Hong Kong the most exciting city in the world. So also are the sounds— clanging streetcars, constant sirens and whistles of cars and emergency vehicles, and the low throbbing of fog horns that make one constantly aware of the harbor that serves as the heart of Hong Kong and the home of the Star Ferry.

If you want to understand global business, a trip to Hong Kong is a required course. Hong Kong is both the introductory course and an advanced graduate seminar in the whys and ways of international business. When I began the chapters for this book, it was titled *From the Edge* to reflect the countries I needed to visit to conduct research for the book and for a new course on global marketing at Ohio State. In the case of Hong Kong, "From the Edge" has even more meaning. It is the edge and entry for some of the fastest growing markets—to sell or to source—in the world.

85

## *Gateway to the Orient*

Hong Kong sits on the edge of the Orient, the key access to China. That massive dragon may have slumbered for decades, but today China is awakening. One of my students at Ohio State completed his doctoral dissertation by interviewing managers throughout China. He found that the two countries with which Chinese *least* desire to do business are Japan and Russia. The two countries the Chinese *most* desire to do business with are Singapore and the United States.

Why should American firms be interested in studying Hong Kong? Because Hong Kong is the gateway to the billion or so consumers who want to buy products and services from many firms. Refrigerators are desired by the Chinese more than any other durable product. Americans, we hope, will find some way to supply this demand or at least some of the components to be assembled in appliances built in China. The folks who know how to find those markets are probably in Hong Kong.

The Chinese want medical equipment. This is a tremendous opportunity for U.S. firms of all types. Some of these will be low- or medium-technology products, but probably the best markets are for high-technology, medically related products. The economy of China may support purchase of some of those products but probably not the research and development funds for manufacture in China. The answer: look to Hong Kong for firms that understand the demand for such products and how to distribute them in China.

Beer is increasingly popular throughout the Orient. That may mean markets through the Hong Kong connection for the cylinders made by Worthington Industries, one of the firms Tom Peters has written about as among the best managed in America. Whatever the products that American firms want to sell in China—and the potential is unlimited—the door to those sales often will first be opened, either directly or indirectly, in Hong Kong. That is the way it has been in the past and will continue to be for quite a while.

South China is a consumption and manufacturing area accessed mostly through Hong Kong. The area contains more than 250 million people—more than the entire United States! Hong Kong companies employ more than 3 million workers in the neighboring southern Chinese province of Kwangtung. Many more commute each day to jobs in Hong Kong.

## *Hong Kong: "Panda-er" to Retailers*

Perhaps pandas are the best known export of China for American animal lovers. When zoos display pandas, the zoos are mobbed with demands from thousands of zoo consumers. But the Hong Kong merchants reflect their heritage more profitably by their "pandaering" to retailers around the world, especially in the apparel business. They are exporting a lot of what we wear—much of it manufactured in China but moving through Hong Kong. Hong Kong is as important to retailers in attracting consumers as pandas are for zoos.

A segment of Americans know well the way to Hong Kong. Those people are the buyers who work for retailers—firms such as the Gap, Paul Harris Stores, or the Limited.

You can be sure that buyers at leading retailers such as the Limited—as well as finance people, computer specialists, logisticians, and nearly everyone else who supports the supply line to the Limited—know Hong Kong well. That is what Hong Kong does best—make things efficiently and distribute them rapidly to retailers all over the world. When you see a 747 at Port Columbus, it is probably unloading clothing from Hong Kong destined eventually for one of the Limited's 3,700 stores.

Hong Kong once thrived because of its cheap labor. Today its success is much more complex. In computer-assisted-design (CAD) and computer-assisted-manufacturing (CAM) systems, Hong Kong is ahead of most U.S. firms. When state-of-the-art technology is combined with relatively low wage rates, Hong Kong achieves a synergy with which many U.S. firms do not compete and probably do not even understand. In a city as computer oriented as Hong Kong, there should be a lot of opportunities for American firms if they can produce state-of-the-art applications software and systems services.

But any firm from another country had better be customer oriented if it hopes to sell in Hong Kong, because Hong Kong merchants and manufacturers are the masters at meeting and exceeding customer expectations.

### *In Hong Kong, You Can Buy Anything—Almost!*

Hong Kong most of all is a city of contrasts: some of the tallest skyscrapers in the world jutting out from sea level; state-of-the-art computers driving super-sophisticated CAD-CAM systems across from a shop toting up sales with an abacus; the finest of European and Chinese cuisine in the best hotels in the world a block away from an open market slaughtering pigs and frogs; the most vibrant and thriving marketplace of capitalists in the world sitting at the edge of the last bastion of communism.

It is said that you can buy anything in the world in Hong Kong—except another century of free market capitalism. The century ends in 1997 when the British cede the colony back to China. The year 1997 hangs over Hong Kong like the cloud that often obscures Victoria Peak.

### *Beyond 1997*

What will the future bring for Hong Kong? After a decade of pessimism, Hong Kong's citizens became optimistic when the Chinese promised Hong Kong would continue its capitalistic role. After all, Beijing needs the jobs, taxes, and currency generated by Hong Kong! The massacre of hundreds of liberation activists at Tiananmen Square in 1989 caused pessimism to return. But in my most recent trip, I saw optimism surfacing again. The stock market has soared. Construction of apartments and office buildings is skyrocketing. Residential apartments have doubled in price.

Hong Kong is one of the major banking centers in the world—probably a logical buyer of the most innovative American banking products. The most innovative approaches to banking in the United States usually originate with Bank One—inventor of the ATM, cash management accounts, drive-in banking, home banking, and point-of-sale equipment for bank cards. Bank One has grown from a small county bank to one of the most profitable banks in the world and one of the largest in the United States by constantly focusing on consumers and developing banking products that are innovative. One of those was BankAmericard, which evolved into VISA and MasterCard. Bank One's expertise in bank cards established its position as the premier developer of computer systems for bank cards. Already Bank One markets those in Mexico and Europe. It would be natural to access all of Asia with a strategic alliance with one of the excellent banks in Hong Kong. These are the kinds of opportunities for American firms to continue their growth that I observe in almost every country I study.

American firms have many other opportunities. U.S. developers, architects, and engineers live in a low-growth environment in the United States because we are in a low-growth population mode. But that is not true in Hong Kong. The Galbreath Management Corporation, based in Columbus, has been described as the builder of the largest apartment complex in the world—and it is in Hong Kong. If you fly into Kai Tak airport in Hong Kong, you feel as if you can almost look inside some of the apartments in this massive complex on every approach to Hong Kong.

Kowloon Airport—one of the most exciting airports in the world because of the spectacular views into the kitchens of nearby apartments—will give way to Chek Lap Kok Airport in 1997, capable of handling 80 million passengers a year (compared to 28 million at Kowloon). This is the kind of opportunity that exists for construction firms or aviation firms that are struggling to find growth domestically. If such firms are capable of thinking globally, they can participate in projects that not only involve airplanes and airports but the new trains, highways, bridges, tunnels, and a ferry to support the intermodal transportation and communications complex.

The United States is home to some of the most outstanding architectural firms. But you will rarely find more innovative architecture than in Hong Kong. I. M. Pei's masterpiece is the dramatic Bank of China Tower. One of the most controversial is the gigantic headquarters of the Hong Kong and Shanghai Bank, designed by Norman Foster. Remo Riva's Exchange Square challenges the imagination with its distinctive curves and hints of art nouveau. Most of the buildings are works of art except for one. It is a tall, square building with nothing but rows of round windows, similar to portholes in ships. A Hong Kong executive told me with a chuckle that it is called the building of ten thousand assholes! One look at the building and you would readily understand why.

No one is sure what 1997 will bring. Many European and other firms are establishing headquarters or major regional offices in Singapore to prepare for any eventuality that would require them to access the Orient from a city other than Hong Kong. On my last trip to Hong Kong, one executive commented that in contrast to firms from other countries, American firms were still mostly locating in Hong Kong. That worried the Hong Kong executive, he said, "Because when it comes to international decisions, Americans always get it wrong."

I hope he is wrong. There is plenty of opportunity left in Hong Kong, as well as plenty in Singapore. It is difficult to predict the long-term future for Hong Kong. In the short run, I do not think there will be much change because of China's need for the infrastructure and financial resources of Hong Kong. And in the long run, I think China will change so much that it will become much like Hong Kong. Those are two of the reasons I am bullish on Hong Kong.

From bargain markets (above) to exclusive retailers (next page), Hong Kong is a shopper's haven

## Shop 'Til You Drop

Oh yes, how can you write about Hong Kong without mentioning shopping? It is still great but the savings are more difficult to find than in the past. They are to be found in Cat Street's flea market or Jardine's Bazaar for cosmetics and ladies' accessories. Go to Stanley Market for the best bargains in clothing. As for cameras, you may do better on Forty-seventh Street in New York.

You can also shop high-fashion retailers, if you so desire. Although never easy on the budget, Escada and Boss retail stores, just to name a few, offer great savings on their latest fashions—or so my wife tells me. But if you do shop those stores, I find it better to

91

think of the dollars you save by buying in Hong Kong rather than at home, instead of thinking of the actual dollars you spend. I'm sure all of you have used this rationale at one time or another.

Every student of marketing needs to spend a few days shopping in Hong Kong. It is the ultimate pricing simulation. If you can negotiate prices well in Hong Kong, you should do well in the rest of your business career, at least with the pricing component of the marketing mix.

The Chinese culture has produced some of the best merchants in the world for products of all types from jade to air conditioners. In the United States, haggling over price is mostly limited to business-to-business marketing. How would K-Mart deal with a culture that expected haggling over every item sold in the store by every consumer? Yet, that is pretty much the situation in Hong Kong.

Once I knew exactly what I wanted and thought the marked price was fair, I told the proprietor I would buy the item. She was offended that I did not haggle over price. "Why don't you ask about price?" she said. "Did I do something wrong?"

What would happen if we did it this way in the United States? Maybe retailing firms could achieve overall higher margins. Perhaps, also, individuals with more negotiating skills could achieve a higher standard of living than those with less marketing ability. It would certainly change some of the attributes we look for in employees.

We do have some firms that apply this principle. Auto dealers, of course, often expect people to deal. The informal sector of the economy—flea markets, garage sales, and other remarketing institutions—is also an area in which variable pricing and negotiation are fairly common. The principle can be found in some large, publicly held firms. Sun TV—a fast-growing, regional appliance retailer—has achieved growth and impressive gains in its stock price with aggressive pricing of the Hong Kong variety.

## *Wear Your Dark Glasses!*

Lately, the marketing profession has shown considerable interest in physiological measures of consumer response. Careful experiments are being conducted in the laboratories of universities and advertising agencies. Some of the equipment used includes Galvanic Skin Response (GSR), Electro Encephalograph (EEG), and Pupil Dilation Response (PDR).

The last one, PDR, uses infrared beams reflected on the pupil of consumers watching ads to measure information processing—or what is commonly called interest in the ad. Where, you might ask, did professors get the idea of watching people's pupils to measure consumer interest in products?

The answer? From Hong Kong jade merchants. Their lives apparently are about as boring as professors' lives. Over the centuries, the jade merchants learned to watch the eyes of consumers. They would spread beautiful jewels on a pad of velvet. As the potential customer looked at the various pieces of jewelry, the merchant studied the person's pupils and noted reactions. The size of the pupil allegedly reflected the interest of the customer in the piece—which, in turn, allegedly affected the price the merchant would ask for the pieces of most interest to the customer. You can still observe this fascinating process in many of the jade shops of Hong Kong. This is why I always wear sunglasses when entering Hong Kong jewelry shops!

Hong Kong is one of the most romantic cities in the world. The harbor at night is enchanting, whether from the shore or from a boat. The restaurants and hotels are by almost any standard the best in the world. If you prefer, however, you can also find Wendy's, Pizza Hut, and Mrs. Fields cookies to quiet hunger pangs for what some people call traditional American cuisine. Romance is real in Hong Kong but still plays second fiddle to business.

Hong Kong lives on business, and maybe that is one of the reasons I view it as the most exciting city in the world. The city never stops. Las Vegas is also described as a twenty-four-hour, neon-lit city but it contains a different type of excitement. Hong Kong offers a different form of hustling than in Las Vegas but far more useful—and in my judgment, far more fun.

In Hong Kong, activity is as continual as the slot machines of Las Vegas, but in Hong Kong the blood that keeps the city going is not gambling. It is business.

That's the way I see it . . . from the edge of the Orient.

# 8

# CHINA

*The Great Wall Is Now a Bridge*

**The Great Wall of China was built** to keep people out. It offered protection from the Mongolian hordes. Today, the Great Wall is China's greatest magnet, attracting hordes of tourists and other visitors.

The exchange that occurs between Chinese people and the country's visitors is an important bridge between the past and the future of China. Not only do visitors bring badly needed currency; they also bring ideas and methods.

## The Most Important Import

As important as the money tourism brings, nothing has had the impact of the ideas that have been imported to China in recent years. Chief among the new ideas is the philosophy of a market-based economy.

Work ethic and respect for culture are important parts of China's dynasty

That idea is catapulting China from an undeveloped, agricultural past not much different from six thousand years ago toward a manufacturing and service-oriented society. China is headed in the direction of being (with a long way to go) a powerhouse economy of the future. The experiment going on in China today can be loosely described as free-market communism.

China is escaping from communism in the opposite manner from the former U.S.S.R. The Soviet Union changed its political structure before changing its economic structure. China is changing its economic structure before changing its political structure. This may be the better way.

A market of more than a billion people is the eye-popping reason many businesses have their eyes on China. One such business is

McDonald's. I enjoyed getting a Big Mac in the middle of Beijing at the store that replaced Moscow's as the world's largest McDonald's. There must be something significant in the fact that McDonald's arches—one of the great symbols of capitalism—are found in the capitals of communism above McDonald's two largest restaurants.

## Marketing with a Past

Some provinces of China ultimately will be more prosperous than most of the former Soviet republics. A major reason is that China has a trading history, an entrepreneurial culture. Even under the Czars, Russia did not have much of a trading and distribution culture. In both China and Russia, trade and distribution were repressed. In today's China, however, there is a substantial trading or marketing orientation to build on. It is much easier to have good marketing in a country with a past history of a trading or marketing culture.

The best merchants in the Orient are often of Chinese origin. If you want to see this firsthand, visit the Silk Market in Beijing. The bargains on clothing and other textile products are outstanding. Quality is high, prices are low, and the merchants are dealin' in ways that would even impress Ford dealer Fred Ricart, who built a small firm into America's largest car dealership with the advertising slogan, "We're Dealin'." The Chinese will do well in modern marketing, partly because of their history of doing deals very well.

## New Meanings for the Concept of Logistics

Beijing has an estimated 10 million people and 8 million bicycles. The reverse appears more likely because every person seems to be on a bicycle and yet there are parking lots covered with thousands more bicycles. The contrasts of China were illustrated well as I was riding in a comfortable Nissan taxi surrounded by bicycles carrying, in addition to people, every other imaginable cargo.

# CHINA
## The Great Wall Is Now a Bridge

A country of bicycles

Bicycles pull wagons covered with food, bricks, equipment, or cases of Coke. One of the more colorful was a bicycle pedaling beside my taxi with nearly a dozen freshly slaughtered chickens hanging by their necks from the handlebar. The use of bicycles to the extent they are used in China gives a meaning to the word logistics quite a bit different from what we are used to in the United States.

The Chinese government has recently proposed limiting the use of bicycles on streets. I can understand the concern about mixing bicycles and cars in bustling city streets, especially when bicycles outnumber the cars by a large multiple. In a developing country, however, pollution and environmental problems are often ignored because of the more pressing concerns for increased economic activity. Bicycles do not pollute and they are a healthy, efficient

A shipment of poultry headed for market

method of transportation. It will be sad to see bicycles give way to cars, even though it is probably inevitable that they will. I can't help but wonder if Los Angeles and New York would not be better cities if they had a lot more bicycles than cars.

## How Many People?

Being an only child is the norm in China. An astounding 93 percent of babies born last year in urban areas were only children. Officially, that should be true in rural areas, but the government-mandated one-child policy is often ignored where people believe they can do so. Nevertheless, the one-child policy, later-age marriages, and widespread use of sterilization make China an example to the world that overpopulation in poor countries can be controlled.

The population of China is still growing because of large

numbers of people born in the 1960s. But with the skyrocketing numbers of one-child families, China has reached a replacement rate of reproduction, an accomplishment normally found only in affluent countries. Tragically, the one-child policy is changing the gender ratio. Infanticide, while illegal, is often found among couples who prefer a male child when they can have only one. One of the major keys to increasing per capita income in China, however, is limiting the number of children. Another consequence is that sometime during the next century, India will probably surpass China as the largest nation in the world.

Since higher levels of personal achievement, greater creativity, fewer personality disorders, and other results of being an only child have been reported in medical and psychology journals, it is interesting to speculate. What will be the effect on a country when most of its children are raised as only children? Sounds like a topic hospital administrator and health reporter Erie Chapman might pursue on a future *LifeChoices*, the nationally syndicated television health show.

## Keep Them Down on the Farm

China is overwhelmingly rural. Nearly 80 percent of the people live on the farm, growing each day what they will eat the next day. Much of this huge country (3,400 miles from north to south and 3,100 miles from east to west) is sparsely populated.

The Tibetan highlands and Xinjian-Mongolia region of western China have 41 percent of China's land mass but only 1 percent of its population. Urban residency is considered a privilege with enormous legal and administrative implications. Population movements between urban and rural areas or even between cities is as regulated in China as it used to be in South Africa.

It is always good to be reflective about major social problems in any society. Sometimes visiting another country and another culture helps put our own culture, as well as others, in perspective. Poor people usually want to move to areas of rich people. That principle leads to migration from farm to city as well as from country to country. Is it better to allow this or to limit such movements?

If we look at many of our problems in the United States, they seem to be accentuated in urban areas. Poverty, crime, and poor housing all seem to have greater effects on urban people than rural people as well as being more likely to occur in large concentrations of people in cities. I wonder if the homeless problem would be as great if we moved a portion of the homeless to abandoned military bases in rural areas and if we moved homeless families with children to small towns where children could have fresh air, country-grown food, and modest but low-priced housing. Many small towns are faced with abandoned homes and stores that reflect the substantial overcapacity to handle their population that exists in small towns and rural areas. Large cities are faced with many more people than we have homes. Small towns are faced with abandoned homes and declining populations, as well as much lower costs of living. There probably are some solutions for some of our problems somewhere in this imbalance.

I realize that restricting mobility presents major civil rights issues that we would not want to face in the United States. Yet in China you can observe a country that recognizes that most people are better off if they are not allowed to move to cities until jobs and housing are available for them. Perhaps restricting urban migration is not a good policy, but it certainly stimulates one to think more critically about our own social problems in the United States.

## Business Is Booming

To say business is booming in a Communist country is a strange idea for many people. Although the term *booming* is an exaggeration for most provinces and totally wrong in some areas of China, business is exploding in some regions in both everyday practice and political acceptance. Those areas provide opportunities for firms based in Japan, Europe, and perhaps North America.

On three, say "Ronald McDonald"

For business firms interested in manufacturing, Northeast China is the center of heavy industry, supplied by the region's ample reserves of coal and ferrous ores as well as oil fields and hydroelectric power. North China produces wheat and other crops in such abundance that China is now an exporter of several agricultural products.

Beijing is such a progressive city that it even has a McDonald's—the world's contemporary benchmark for economic success! I must admit it was a welcome sight after days of suffering from Mac attack symptoms. It was there that I saw one of Beijing's most loved local attractions. The line of children waiting to sit in the lap of a Ronald McDonald statue was longer than most American amusement park queues. The parents waited patiently so they could snap pictures of their children with a piece of Americana.

American firms interested in low-priced textiles, steel, and machinery will find plenty of sources in the cities of Tientsin, Tangshan, and Beijing. If you are a reader of old maps, you may still refer to Beijing as Peking. For some reason, however, "Beijing Duck" still lacks the culinary appeal of Peking Duck!

The biggest attraction to globally oriented business firms is probably Kuang-chou, formerly known as Canton, best known to Americans for Cantonese-style food. South China and the Kwangtung area are also the manufacturing source of many of the products that are found in almost every American store, whether it be the Limited, Lazarus, or Odd Lots. Many of the goods move through Shanghai, China's largest city and most important port.

Does China have one language or many? The answer is yes. While China has one uniform written language, its pronunciation differs so much from area to area that it is more realistically considered many languages. Mandarin (from the Beijing area) is dominant, the official diplomatic language, and the one to learn if you are serious about doing business in China. Cantonese, however, is dominant in nearby Hong Kong and probably more familiar to most Americans.

China's businesses, at least the large ones and even most retail firms, are still very much owned and controlled by the government. When Sheraton, Westin, Marriott, Hyatt, or other American-based firms open in China (and many are doing so), the buildings are built and owned by the government. You can imagine the problems of bureaucracy that are created by state ownership. This gives true meaning to the term *red tape*!

As I traveled through China, I could not help but wonder if America's leader in budget motels, Red Roof Inns, might not be the most logical partner for a communist country! The red tape is substantial but for the persistent business partner, the rewards of operating in China are worth the effort.

# CHINA
*The Great Wall Is Now a Bridge*

## *If You've Got the Money, China Has the Goods*

China has changed in many ways since my first trip several years ago. The most striking change is the availability of anything you might want to buy. The "starving children of China" that my mother cited when she admonished me to eat everything on my plate are no longer common. Food is relatively abundant. Everything is now available to buy for anyone who has the money.

Most people have very little money, however. My wife and I visited factories where people with connections get "good jobs." These "good jobs" require a person to work six days a week for ten or twelve hours a day for about sixty dollars a month. Many people work seven days a week and get a total of seven days vacation for the year.

Housing is extremely scarce. Young people in the cities must wait decades before they can get an apartment, usually spending most of their lives sharing the small apartment of parents who have been fortunate enough to have a factory job for many years.

## *What Do They Really Want?*

What products do the Chinese own or want to buy? Bicycles, watches, radios, sewing machines, cameras, refrigerators, and televisions are the most popular, but demand for those products is concentrated in urban areas. Television ownership is high, with at least 75 percent owning a television—rather amazing when one considers that a typical set costs about 75 percent of the typical per capita income for a year!

Private cars are still just a dream and probably not even that for most people for many years. The vehicles that are sold in China are mostly trucks or commercial vehicles. With limited exceptions in the special economic zones, autos are almost always owned by corporations. Although trade regulations are the same for the United States and Japan, most of the cars and trucks that I saw in China were made and marketed by the Japanese.

# CHINA
## The Great Wall Is Now a Bridge

Once more, I became convinced that the problem of American auto manufacturers is not Japan's trade barriers. The problem is American management's inability to think globally. The problems of American auto firms include the inability to manufacture efficiently, and labor unions have to take their share of blame for the problem. The problems of American firms also include the historical weakness (with some recent improvement) to market worldwide with the long-range planning and cross-cultural understanding of Japanese firms.

The greatest opportunities for U.S. firms to sell in China are in the areas of technology—computers and software, industrial machinery, and so forth. The firms that are successful in selling must usually be successful also in counter trade—finding outlets for the products that can be made with the equipment.

The biggest product China has for sale is labor. Basically, labor is traded to U.S. firms that can supply machinery, technology, and management. Effective management in firms must also find worldwide markets for the products made with Chinese labor.

During the rapid appreciation of the yen in recent years, the Japanese have been big investors in China also. They are investing in factories in a way different from most other countries. In addition to investing in factories to build export goods, the Japanese are building factories in China to produce goods that will be sold in China.

But there is good news for American firms. One of my Ph.D. students at Ohio State completed his dissertation by interviewing more than one hundred Chinese managers. He found that the most favored trading partners were the United States and Singapore. The least favored or trusted were the Japanese and the Russians.

## A Tourist Paradise

Americans are flocking to China in large numbers. And for good reason. Some of the most fascinating tourist sights in the world are in China. The Great Wall is the most popular of them all, and it is amazing. I enjoyed jogging on the wall, although it was only to be able to say that I had jogged on the Great Wall. It was too crowded for a serious jog except, I am told, during the Great Wall Marathon.

Some of the most delightful hours I spent in China—or anywhere—were in the Beijing Zoo. You can guess where I spent most of my time—at the panda compound. Whenever pandas are displayed in zoos around the world, they attract huge crowds and usually there is only a limited amount of time to see them. But in Beijing, you can stay as long as you like in relatively uncrowded conditions. You can walk through and around the building and see many families of pandas frolicking, eating, and sleeping.

My wife and I were totally charmed by the bear-like pandas. Koalas dozing in Australia. Stately mother giraffes grazing with their babies on the plains of Africa. These are some of my favorite animals. But none is so totally fascinating—and so endangered—as the pandas in China.

The Forbidden City is incomprehensible unless you actually see it. I had seen it portrayed in textbooks and in movies, most notably *The Last Emperor*. I still was not prepared for the enormity of the Forbidden City.

As you can see by reading this book, generally I am sparse in my comments about tourist attractions when describing most countries. I hesitate to recommend tourist attractions because I think it is much more important to get to know the people and their culture in a country.

The Forbidden City is an exception. It is a people and their culture. I can't explain it. It is a history lesson, a philosophy lesson, and an anthropology lesson all encompassed in one massive city within a city. It even comes with a portable cassette player and a guided tour tape in your favorite language! When you go to the Forbidden City, I recommend the self-paced cassette tour for a beginning overview.

If you have to save money for years to be able to go to China, do it. And don't miss the Forbidden City!

## *A Final Tip*

For the world traveler with appreciation for the past and a vision for the future, China is a must. Not only are the people generally pro-American, they are almost always helpful and courteous. There are many problems in arranging transportation, but with proper planning, Americans will find travel in China generally easy, at least if they stay near to Western-managed hotels and do not try to change their airline reservations.

If you are like me, you want to visit the same stores and markets that are patronized by the local people. You learn a lot about their lifestyles that way. Visitors can also shop at Friendship stores, which are bountifully stocked with everything you need from both the eastern and the western world, usually at attractive prices. The Friendship stores are worth a visit.

And here is a final tip. You are not supposed to tip anyone. It is officially discouraged by the government and not expected as a condition for good service. And a country where tipping is prohibited or discouraged has to be considered a wonderful country to visit!

That's the way I see it . . . from the edge.

# 9

# SWITZERLAND

*From the Top of the World*

**Would you want to live in a country** slightly more than one-third the size of Ohio? How successful is that country likely to be if it is so multicultural that it is composed of three different nationalities and cultures and three different languages? Add to that a fourth language as the official language of the country—with almost no one knowing how to speak it—and another language that is not officially accepted, yet nearly everyone speaks it.

What is the standard of living likely to be in such a country? Especially when you learn that it has no natural resources, no access to major waterways, very little land for agriculture, and is frozen over with snow much of the year. Would you guess that the people would be among the most impoverished in the world? Or among the richest in the world?

A country of diverse people, activities, and languages

Add to the country's challenges that it is more than 70 percent mountains and has no economic or military alliances with
other countries that might be called upon to help in an emergency.
Throw in the fact that religious rivalries date back centuries and
were led by influential theologians, some of whom believed in con-
version at the point of a sword!

By now you probably have guessed that the country is Switzerland. Perhaps you also know that consistently, decade after decade, Switzerland is one of the richest nations on a per capita basis
of any of the world. Surely, people in the United States would want
to seek the reason why Switzerland has such high per capita GDP in
order to learn some lessons that could be applied to our own ailing

economy. In my visits to countries around the world in preparation for this book, Switzerland proved to be one of the most instructive.

## *Why Are People Rich or Poor?*

Why is one country rich and another poor? If you think back to a high school geography class, perhaps someone told you the wealth of a country is based on natural resources. Although there are a few temporary exceptions in the oil-rich countries of the Middle East, the natural resource theory doesn't hold up when you visit countries such as Argentina, Brazil, and Nigeria—or even Russia.

The countries with the highest per capita natural resources are among the poorest in the world. Countries with almost no natural resources, not even farmland—such as Switzerland and Japan—are among the richest in the world. Don't you find it interesting that the largest food company in the world—Nestle—is based in one of the world's smallest countries? So are some the world's most powerful banks, pharmaceutical and equipment manufacturing firms.

The reason people in one country are rich and the people in another country are poor is not capital—that flows around the world in an instant today. The poor entrepreneur in Thailand or Korea can obtain capital from German, U.S., or Japanese bankers who want to invest in such countries. Today the transfer of capital is measured in nanoseconds. Capital transfer is almost as rapid to the entrepreneur in a poor country as it is to one in a capital-rich country.

## *Values*

The reason resource-starved countries such as Switzerland, Japan, and Singapore rank among the richest in the world is their values. That principle probably holds for organizations and individuals as well. The difference between a Wal-Mart and its competitors is not its products or prices, for those can be found in other stores; it is values—of its management and employees. In the case of Wal-Mart, many of those values can be traced directly to its founder, Sam Walton, and his successor and fellow Missourian, David Glasser.

If there is one principle I wish entrepreneurs, stockholders, managers, and those who wish to be in each of those categories understood, it is this: The long-term success of any firm, especially in the slow-growth environment of highly industrialized countries, is more determined by a firm's values than any of its other resources. The corporate culture is as important as a country's culture.

If you go to Switzerland, the most important thing to see is not the Matterhorn—as inspiring as that great mountain is. Look most and longest at the values that make Switzerland one of the most likely places in the world for a person or corporation to be financially successful.

What values will you observe in Switzerland? Cleanliness, organization, discipline, respect for God and family, excellence in national defense capability, financial conservatism, respect for people with different languages and different cultures (but not to the point of adopting their ineffective values), no waste, and hard work.

Those are some of the values that allow people in Switzerland to have such a high standard of living. Probably anyone in any country can also be prosperous, but not without understanding values such as those of the Swiss.

## *It Is Very Important to Wash before Eating*

The Association for Consumer Research was founded at The Ohio State University in the late 1960s. Some of the most influential researchers in the field met to consider what was known at that time about consumer behavior. One of the papers that made an impression on me and others was by Dr. William Wells, a pioneer in consumer behavior and marketing research. His paper was about predicting behavior with the use of psychographics. One of the psychographic or AIO (Activity, Interest, Opinion) statements most useful in predicting behavior became the name of that early research paper: "It Is Very Important to Wash before Eating."

Cleanliness may not be the most important value in determining prosperity, but it is one of the most visible in Switzerland. Successful people and successful firms today need to know and practice many values—but lack of cleanliness is a visible sign indicating that unsuccessful people do not have a clue about what is required for success. Perhaps it is discipline, consideration of others, organization, or other values that actually lead to prosperity, but cleanliness is externally visible evidence that an individual or a society understands what is required to be successful.

In Switzerland, the hotels and restaurants sparkle as much as the snow-washed mountain peaks. Some young Swiss may have long hair—but not dirty long hair! Both rich people and poor people can be clean. But poor people normally should not expect to become rich until they first become clean. Lotteries and rock stars may provide exceptions to the rule, but "be clean" is good advice for those who want to be prosperous.

American businesses can learn from the Swiss. One place the cleanliness principle can be practiced is in rest rooms. I subscribe to the rest room theory of management! Show me a firm with dirty rest rooms and I will show you a firm with poor customer service, low-quality products, and probably dirty accounting as well! Visiting a country such as Switzerland makes such principles easy to see.

The *International Herald-Tribune* once published an article about my conclusions concerning cleanliness. The article described me as the father of the "Rest Room Theory of Management." I am not sure that is the epitaph I would want on my tombstone, but the more I travel and observe prosperous and impoverished people, the more it is empirically obvious. Do not expect to be prosperous if you cannot learn to be clean. Some people might argue that poor people cannot afford to be clean but I don't agree. Soap does not cost much!

## *The Best Offense Is a Good Defense*

One of the things you probably will not see in Switzerland is its defense system. But it is omnipresent nevertheless. It is underground with an intricate system of tunnels, supply depots, under-the-mountain airfields, and command posts capable of surviving nuclear attack.

All citizens participate in the defense system until they are in their fifties. Much of the management structure of Swiss businesses is closely related to the military defense system. A person who is disloyal or uninvolved in the defense of the country is unlikely to succeed in business. A Swiss friend of mine emigrated to the United States. He had been dishonorably discharged from the Swiss military and told me that a business career in Switzerland would therefore be nearly impossible.

Switzerland has little if any offensive capability, but it probably has the most sophisticated, secret, and effective defense system in the world. Switzerland has never chosen the role of being a global cop, as the United States has. Far from being considered the coward of the county, as Kenny Rogers once sang about, Switzerland has maintained such strength that neither Germany, the U.S.S.R., nor any other country believed it could mess with Switzerland. Neutrality, or the unwillingness to impose one's moral beliefs on others, is a value that is condemned by many people. It is difficult, however, to deny that it is one of the values that has contributed to Switzerland's prosperity.

Does the fact that most Swiss citizens participate in a highly structured military defense system affect the effectiveness of its business organizations? Quite possibly, and it raises questions about what has been happening in the United States in recent years.

With the great concern that exists about the U.S. budget deficit, it is natural to look for places to cut spending. The defense system is an obvious choice, especially with the demise of the cold war between the United States and Communist nations. Yet, if you asked what government program has been the most effective in changing the status of disadvantaged individuals and groups in this country, I think most people would answer that it is the military.

While prejudice and discrimination are still rampant throughout the United States (and almost every other country in the world), the large U.S. organization that probably has the best record for promotion of people to the top on the basis of merit rather than color or national origin is the U.S. military. The last two commanding generals of the Joint Chiefs of Staff have been General Colin Powell, an American of African cultural background, and General John "Shali" Shalikashvili, a Polish-born person of Georgian and German heritage. I'm not convinced that either would have been as successful in organizations that were more discriminatory than the military.

If any large organization is good at training persons from disadvantaged backgrounds into high-tech jobs with managerial responsibilities, it is the U.S. Army. In the interest of reducing defense expenditures, a goal most people believe worthwhile, we are downsizing dramatically an organization that has been very effective at creating jobs for people from all backgrounds, promoting on merit rather than discrimination (at least more than most organizations), and developing high levels of modern technological capability, often with people without much advanced education. Additionally, many officers and enlisted people have been so effectively trained in the military that they have received excellent positions in airlines, computer, and communications firms and many other businesses after leaving the military.

It makes you wonder if the job creation and training programs being proposed by the government will be as effective in accomplishing those same goals, doesn't it? When I saw how important the military was in Switzerland to developing a disciplined, trained, loyal work force, it caused me to consider our own situation a little more thoroughly than I might otherwise have done.

## *Value-Added Values*

Several other values make the Swiss among the richest people in the world despite their lack of natural resources. One value is optimistic hard work that produces the skill and determination to produce products with much higher value than do societies blessed with natural resources.

The Swiss do not have much land for their cows, so they take the milk they do have and convert it into high-value cheese. They do not have iron ore and great steel mills, so they put people to work in small villages producing steel that can be sold for thousands of dollars per pound—as the world's finest watches.

The Swiss do not have any gold, so they developed a banking system, backed by governmental policies and the strong defense system, that causes a large part of the gold in the rest of the world to be left on deposit in Switzerland. They do not have large computer manufacturers, so they develop computerized information systems that handle a large portion of the world's financial transactions. They do not have oil, so they buy it from commodity-producing nations and convert it to some of the most advanced pharmaceutical products in the world.

I cannot believe that the Swiss are born with better genes than people who live in countries that produce only commodities have. I do believe Swiss citizens grow up in an environment of better values than most other countries.

## *Grow Your Own Prosperity*

Every home in Switzerland has a garden—often in the area Americans use as a front lawn. Because of the climate, they grow vegetables such as cabbage that survive cold temperatures well into the autumn.

Most Americans protest that we do not have time to work in

gardens. Or perhaps we think lawns are prettier than gardens. Someone calculated that if the fertilizer used on American lawns were used for agricultural purposes, more food could be produced than the amount needed to feed all the starving people in the world.

Middle-class Americans decide to spend their time, scarce water, and expensive fertilizer on lawns—and complain about the high cost of groceries and the inability to build a large savings account in the bank. The Swiss spend those same resources growing food in the back and front yards and save lots of money, making more money for both themselves and the Swiss banks. Literally, the Swiss grow their own prosperity.

## *Waste Not, Want Not*

Visiting Switzerland allows you to see how wasteful Americans are. Go to an American supermarket and you will still see many people receiving paper or plastic bags to carry the groceries—and ultimately to fill up landfills. Expecting supermarkets to supply bags to customers would generally be unthinkable for the Swiss. Walk into any supermarket or observe people walking home and you will notice that the Swiss (and many other Europeans) take reusable bags to the supermarket to carry home the groceries. True, some Americans do the same thing, but not many compared to Swiss consumers.

Everywhere you look, it is possible to see the anti-waste values of the Swiss. Recycling stations are everywhere. When vegetables are peeled or cut, nothing is wasted. All parts of an animal are used for food. Every inch of farmland is used—right to the road. Vineyards are planted up and down the hills to use every available inch. Americans might protest and say it is not efficient to use every inch of the mountain because heavy farm machinery cannot be used. The Swiss solve that problem with manual labor from dawn to dark—by every member of the family.

Hard work. Use every part of every resource. Waste not, want not. It is not difficult to understand why the Swiss have such a high standard of living.

## *Love of Family*

The Swiss work hard. But they also enjoy life—with good food, good drink, good holidays, and great festivals.

Love of family is also something that can be seen everywhere in Switzerland. Look closely at family activities and you will often see multigenerational groupings. It is not uncommon for daughters to stroll arm in arm with their parents for long walks around the lakes and trees. Grandparents and grandchildren are together constantly. Young people hold open the doors in stores for their elders.

There is the highest of respect for all generations of the family. You can see it everywhere in Switzerland. You also see parents strolling with their children in buggies on Saturday and Sunday afternoons. The Swiss—like most Europeans—love and spend time with their children. Observing closely that value of the Swiss and contrasting it with what you see in the United States may reveal one of the greatest weaknesses of America.

## *Respect for God*

One other value is very apparent in Switzerland—respect for those who seek God. In Switzerland, that generally is done in the Judeo-Christian tradition.

The Sabbath in Jewish sections of Zurich can be spiritually inspiring and impressive to visitors, but perhaps at no time is the respect Swiss have for the God of history more apparent than on Sunday morning. Church bells ring throughout the land. You can hear them across the lakes, through the valleys, in every city and every village. It is truly remarkable that in a country this prosperous, people are so religious.

Swiss religion is a realistic and historically based approach to religion, not some of the super-religiosity seen among American cultish forms of Christianity. And in this land of theologian Ulrich

Zwingli and the other reformers, there is respect for those of different religions, including the active Jewish community as well as others.

In fact the Swiss show great tolerance for people of different religions, different languages, and different dress. But respecting someone different is not the same thing as adopting the values of those who are different.

The Swiss are purists. The values that made the country great are respected so much that few people are allowed to immigrate to Switzerland unless they possess the same values.

## *Lessons Learned*

What makes a country great? If it is military power to rule the world, Switzerland would not qualify. Yet its financial conservatism and other values have given it economic power respected by the leaders of every country in the world. The Swiss civil defense system and wealth gave it power that even Hitler's army was unwilling to attack.

A value system that respects hard work, cleanliness, family, God, and disciplined organizations gives Switzerland a prosperity that has survived for centuries.

In America, people are asking about the solutions to many of our problems. Perhaps we need not spend so much time thinking about government programs that would help, as the values that would help. Understanding the Swiss helps us understand that it is not our resources that create success. Success arises from our values.

When people, corporations, or countries are not as successful as they would like to be, perhaps they should study a little country sitting on top of the world. They will find that the key to Switzerland's prosperity is not its natural resources; the key to prosperity is its values.

That's the way I see it . . . from the edge, at the top of the world.

# 10

# SINGAPORE

*Swiss Twin and Key to the Pacific Rim*

**No crime. No poverty. No dirt.** Could that be true for any country in the world? Yes, at least one. Anyone who has been to Singapore might use all of those phrases to describe the city-country that is the heart of the Pacific Rim economic boom. Some might also describe the city as no fun, alluding to its strict rules about anticonformity or most forms of deviant behavior.

If you read the last chapter about Switzerland, I think you will find this chapter similar in many ways. As close to the sea as Switzerland is far away from sea level, as warm as Switzerland is cold, and halfway around the world, Singapore may seem very different from Switzerland. Yet the remarkable similarities between the two small countries cause me to label Singapore and Switzerland as twin nations.

Switzerland has the highest average per capita income in the world. Singapore's is also very high and has grown so dramatically

119

that it is often called the "economic miracle of the Orient." Switzerland and Singapore have both achieved their remarkable prosperity with no oil, no minerals or other natural resources, and very little land. Both Singapore and Switzerland are lands where people who speak different languages, practice different religions, and arise from radically different cultures all make lots of money through banking, entrepreneurship, and a trading economy. And in both countries, especially Singapore, you will find the world's cleanest rest rooms!

## *Small Is Best*

Where would you look to find the best and one of the largest airlines in the world? In a country smaller than Cleveland? You might not expect to find the best airline in the world in one of the smallest countries, but that is exactly where Singapore Airlines has been rated in surveys of international travelers in recent years. (British Airways has also jumped to the top recently.)

Singapore Airlines thrives on outstanding service by outstanding people. It does not get its success from low prices, although it can be as price competitive as any firm when it needs to be. In recent years, U.S. firms and business schools have been stressing Total Quality Management (TQM), customer satisfaction measures, and "outrageously good service." Those concepts are nothing new to Singapore Airlines. They have been its key to prosperity for years, catapulting the tiny regional airline into one of the world's best, largest, and most profitable airlines.

It is difficult to explain just why Singapore Airlines is so successful or how it is different from other airlines, even though my wife and I wrote about the firm in our book *Contemporary Cases in Consumer Behavior*. But people who travel to the Orient and many other destinations of the world consistently report that Singapore Airlines is better on detail after detail. Singapore Airlines provides a level of service in coach that rivals many airlines' service in business or even first class.

# SINGAPORE
## *Swiss Twin and Key to the Pacific Rim*

Singapore's harbor is its gateway to profits

A lesson can be learned from Singapore Airlines. You can be highly profitable by being the best. In recent years, many North American firms have complained that the domestic or world economy has caused them to be unsuccessful. Many of the firms, in my judgment, are not facing up to the hard reality: it is no longer good enough to satisfy customers. In today's environment, the only firms that deserve to prosper and grow are those that know how to delight customers. Singapore Airlines and its people know how to delight the customer!

One of the principles with which businesspeople must grapple is that global competition is best-to-best. When a domestic marketer is competing with other firms, it usually has an array of competitors from very good to very bad. A long time ago, many U.S. firms sent their least competitive products into the export market. When I was a graduate student (many years ago), I remember an in-

Most hotels could only hope to be this manicured

ternational marketing book stating one of the reasons a firm should be interested in international business is to have a place to sell obsolete equipment.

Today it is completely the opposite. Only the best firms export to other countries. When they do export, they send their very best products. Consumers are the beneficiaries of that process, and firms that do not use the best products and services in the world as benchmarks against which to judge their own probably will not be survivors in the modern global economy.

I know that, as a reader, you may not think of yourself in the context of international manufacturing. But that is not the point. Every individual who works for any firm in any line of trade or service must realize that the era of employment in "good" firms is over. Only people who perform with excellence in firms that are excellent are likely to find satisfying employment in the future. The old, easy times of the post–World War II era are over. Mundane, low-paying jobs may still be available for many people, but the only individuals who can expect to have an outstanding career are those who understand how firms such as Singapore Airlines can provide outstanding quality when competitors are struggling in bankruptcy.

There is no longer room for good firms or good employees in the global economy. Among those who seek success, there is room only for excellence.

## Let's Do Lunch in a Changi Rest Room

Singapore caters to everyone from businesspeople to boat bums. And it prospers from them all. More than 24 million people travel to and from Singapore each year, passing through the Changi Airport on more than 1,900 flights a week.

Changi is one of the most remarkable airports in the world. It has all the normal restaurants, duty-free shops, car rental services, and so forth that you would expect. Beyond that, the airport boasts a supermarket, children's play area, cinema, hairdressing salons, nursery, pharmacy, hotel, and a business center complete with first-rate secretarial services. In fact, when you enter the airport lobby and customs areas, you tend to wonder whether you are actually in an airport or in an upscale hotel lobby.

Changi is incredibly efficient for both cargo and passengers. By the time you disembark from the planes and walk the short distance to the baggage carousel, your luggage will be there. Another short walk, together with a very short queue for customs, and you are out of the airport, in an immaculate taxi, and on your way to one of the world's best hotels. Total elapsed time from plane to taxi: typically about seven minutes! Time to the hotel: another ten or fifteen minutes. Always, even in rush hour traffic.

One of the most impressive aspects of Changi Airport is the tall trees lining the road to the airport. With characteristic fore-thought, Singapore officials planted the trees years before the air-

Baggage carousel hidden in a botanical garden

port was opened so they would be just right when the airport was completed. Two of the newest and largest airports in the United States are found in Denver and Pittsburgh. The trees were not quite as tall at the opening of those airports as at Changi.

The most dramatic of all parts of Changi Airport may be the rest rooms. I have seen toilets, loos, water closets, and rest rooms in some of the best restaurants and hotels of the world. None is as clean as those at Changi Airport. The Changi toilets are carpeted, spotless, and have beautiful flowers hanging from the walls—even in the men's toilets! There is rarely a scrap of litter on the floor nor a sniff of odor in any toilet. It is so sparkling clean and so lacking in the normal odoriferous attributes of toilets that you could eat lunch in the rest room.

I have made that comment in front of various audiences of people. Usually, most of the people shake their heads in disbelief or skepticism. As a reader, perhaps that is your reaction. "No rest room is that clean," people often comment—except for a few people in the audience. Sometimes I ask people who agree with my comment about the cleanliness of Changi toilets to explain why. Their answer is usually, "Because I've been there."

Wouldn't it be nice if Americans were as interested in keeping public places as clean as Singaporeans? Frankly, the toilets of Changi are cleaner than the waiting areas or even the restaurants in most American airports.

## And All the Ships at Sea

One of the most amazing photographs I have in my collection was taken from an airplane over Singapore. I wish the quality were high enough to reproduce in this book because it illustrates the health of Singapore's economy as well as any picture could.

The photo portrays the Singapore harbor with several lines of ships extending from the harbor out into the ocean for many miles. If you have ever watched the skies near an airport, you may have seen the lights of dozens of planes in a landing pattern strung across the horizon. It is the same for the Singapore harbor. I was told that more than 250 ships enter the Singapore harbor each day to leave or pick up cargo from nearly every corner of the world.

The logistics capability of the Singapore harbor is arguably the best in the world. Ships are scheduled to arrive and depart on a twenty-four-hour appointment basis. Each ship is cradled into a crane-like apparatus that can load and unload a massive ship in two hours! It appears that all the ships at sea eventually end up at Singapore to be loaded or unloaded.

Logistics management is one of the most important functions in business today. Simply stated, logistics deals with the ability to get the right products to the right place at the right time in the right condition and at the right price. Competency in the logistics function increasingly distinguishes profitable firms from unprofitable ones.

If you are one of those readers who already understands and

appreciates the value of logistics management, go to Singapore and worship at a citadel of logistics efficiency. If you have not yet become a believer in the religion of logistics, let me encourage you to go to Singapore's airport and harbor to get converted. Then come home and curl up with a good logistics textbook!

You will be on your way to prosperity, if you can just keep from going to sleep.

## *The Tropical Silicon Valley*

Singapore is a tropical country located nearly on the equator. Don't worry too much about the heat, however, because every building is air-conditioned. Even the streets seem tolerable because of their shade trees and flowers. Computers control the climate of Singapore's dramatic skyscrapers and housing projects. They control almost everything else, ranging from the flow of traffic on Singapore's carefully regulated freeways to its high-tech fiber optic and satellite networks serving the international banking and insurance community.

Singapore has one of the highest computer literacy rates in the world. This tiny country of about 3 million people is also one of the largest producers of computers (somewhere around sixth or seventh largest) in the entire world. The goal is to have all homes equipped with fiber optic networks and personal computers by the year 2000, and Singapore is well on its way toward achieving that goal.

American firms such as AT&T are putting their highest technology and most advanced manufacturing facilities in Singapore for a simple reason. Singapore may be in the tropics, but the belief in being computer literate by business, government, and ordinary citizens is probably higher than what you would find even in Silicon Valley. That is just one of the reasons that Singapore is becoming the banking and financial center of the Orient, prompting many such firms to move from Hong Kong or Tokyo to the more modern and business-friendly environment of Singapore.

126

## *Health and Education*

What are the education and health care systems like in Singapore? They are exactly as you would expect—world class. Singapore very possibly has the best level of health care for all citizens that exists in the world today.

The educational system is very competitive and first-rate in every respect. And access is strictly on the basis of merit. You can be the child of the richest person in Singapore or the poorest; you can be of any gender, race, or culture. Your access to a first-class education will be dependent on your own personal merit. If you can't make it on merit, you had better hope that your parents are wealthy enough to send you to the United States or some other place where education is more dependent on money than merit.

How does Singapore get the best professors in the world? It invests money in the best people. The very best individuals are identified at a young age, and the state pays for the best education. The best students are sent to the top schools in Singapore and later to the best universities in the world. I was told that the state typically invests $300,000 in preparing a professor to ensure that only the most competent persons become professors and that those people receive the finest education in the world. That is a bit different from the way we do it in the United States.

Singaporeans value education greatly. In the United States, we often take the opposite position in both words and behavior.

Often we show disdain for intelligent people by calling them "nerds" and compensating them unfavorably when compared to athletes or rock musicians. Too many American parents warn their children to avoid "hard" subjects such as mathematics, physics, or foreign languages. Parents and even the media display their true feelings about intellectual activity when they label an idea as unimportant by describing it as "academic."

I know of one American company in which the chief executive officer has taken the position that the human relations department will value quality of education in all of its new hires, for every position in the firm. Recruiters are instructed to look at high school and college records and ask whether the student took easy or hard courses. It should not be the cumulative average of a student that is important but whether that student (probably with the encouragement or discouragement of parents) took rigorous, analytical courses that produce workers and citizens who have the technical, scientific, and behavioral skills to keep a company—and therefore a country—successful in today's competitive, global economy.

Perhaps all of us who are parents should ask ourselves this question: How well have we encouraged and taught our children by example to take the most rigorous courses possible throughout elementary, secondary, and university courses?

Respect and reward for education is the official policy of the Singaporean government. Many, if not most, Singaporean families I have known seem to follow the policy. We probably need to ask ourselves the question, Do our communities and schools place as much emphasis on mathematics and foreign languages as they do on football, cultural understanding, and social relationships?

By any objective comparison, the health care and education systems of Singapore are among the best if not the best in the world. I doubt that Singaporeans are born with genes that produce good doctors and good professors. They live in a culture that places high value on both good health and good education.

## No Poverty

When you have the kind of values that characterize Singapore, there is not much need for either poverty or crime. Good education, good health care, cleanliness, global logistics capability, and a strong spirit of entrepreneurship produce the obvious result: no poverty.

Singapore is a social welfare state based on a strongly capitalistic, market-oriented economy. It is both the ideal and the antithesis of what both liberals and conservatives believe to be the right way to organize society. It achieves most of the lofty goals of utopian socialism but does so with a thoroughly consumer-oriented, market-driven, government-dominated capitalism. Perhaps that is the reason American textbooks with their dichotomous idealism do not understand and therefore generally ignore Singaporean economic and political structures.

It really is true. Very little poverty exists in Singapore. Of course, income and wealth vary. And in some areas of the city, such as Little India, conditions are not so good. For the most part, however, nearly all people have access to good housing, good food, and good health.

Tour Singapore and you will see huge government housing developments. Look at them closely and you will see they are uniformly clean and well maintained. They contain no graffiti, no violence, and no visible vice. One of the reasons is that people who live in government projects have great pride in their homes. The government has devised an ingenious system whereby employers and individuals contribute to a social security type of fund that eventually is used to buy one's own home. The home you rent in the government housing development is the one you will eventually own and retire in. People keep such homes clean. They paint them and they grow flowers and great communities as well.

## Secrets of a Society's Success

It seems that nearly every family is an entrepreneur in Singapore. Winston Churchill once called France a nation of shopkeepers. It is a much more accurate statement about Singapore. Streets are lined with shops selling every imaginable product in the world, facilitated by wholesalers and trading companies that link the ports of the world with Singapore. The shops are clean, charge fair prices, give excellent service, and most often are managed and operated by an entire family. How can you miss having prosperity with a system such as that?

In the United States and other industrialized countries, we increasingly live in an era of nonemployment. We need very few people living and working on farms in order to supply food for Americans today. Our agricultural system is so productive that we are able to feed one thousand Americans with only three working on the farm. The same thing has happened in manufacturing. We need fewer workers in factories today than in 1950, even though we produce many times the output to clothe, house, and feed a vastly increased population. Now the same thing is happening in white collar and managerial jobs.

The simple relationship that is emerging in mature industrialized countries is that we have little economic need for many (my estimate is about 40 percent) of the adults in the traditional employment areas in agriculture, manufacturing, and managerial or professional jobs. Where will we find the greatest growth of meaningful jobs (beyond the low-paying service and retail clerk jobs)?

I am convinced the answer for America and other mature industrialized countries is small business. That is already the answer in Singapore. We can learn a lot about the future of the United States and Canada by studying the present in Singapore.

## No Crime

I have jogged in every country I have visited, with the exception of Peru, as you will read about in chapter 13. I am not very fast and I am certainly not very pretty to watch when I jog. I am afraid I am like President Bill Clinton, who gives jogging a bad image. One of the best ways to understand a city or country, however, is to spend an hour or two jogging through its streets or fields, stopping when the opportunity presents itself for a drink of water and a conversation with the locals.

I can attest to the "no dirt" label for Singapore because of my daily jogs. When plodding along streets and freeways, I never see a candy wrapper, bottle, can, or other litter alongside the road. That is not the normal situation when jogging alongside U.S. highways.

# SINGAPORE
## Swiss Twin and Key to the Pacific Rim

Even cigarette butts are usually deposited in appropriate receptacles in Singapore. Several ashtrays are located in each block, and I have observed that people almost always use them. In only one instance have I seen a Singaporean throw a cigarette butt on the ground, and that was in the driveway of a hotel when a taxi driver was called unexpectedly by the doorman to pick up a guest.

It is prudent when jogging to inquire about the safety of various routes, and I did that in Singapore. One taxi driver assured me that in Singapore you could jog anywhere at any time and never be concerned about muggers or thieves. That is certainly not the answer I would get about Central Park in New York City!

When I asked the driver why there is so little theft or other crime in Singapore, his answer was to the point, "Everybody has enough."

One of the most impressive aspects of Singapore is its lack of crime. It was not always that way. The Tongs—a kind of Chinese Mafia—controlled drugs, prostitution, gambling, and other assorted vices for centuries. Neither the British nor the Japanese could control them or their crime during the rule of each of those colonial powers. But Singapore's great leader, Lee Kuan Yew, did. How? Punishment.

When you enter Singapore, your visa will clearly state that drugs are illegal and that the penalty for violating the law can be death. When I was in Singapore on a previous trip, three people were hanged for selling marijuana. The result: in Singapore you can be a parent and be nearly certain that your children will not grow up with the temptation of drugs or any of the violence that surrounds drug trafficking in the United States and elsewhere.

Perhaps no country in the world has a more objective judicial system or is a better place to get a fair trial. If you are accused of a crime and you are innocent, Singapore provides a legal system likely to find you innocent. But if you are found guilty, Singapore provides a legal system that will provide swift and certain punishment.

Which would you choose? A drug-free, violence-free society with the attendant cost of an occasional death of a person proved

If you want to smoke, be prepared to pay

without a doubt to be a drug dealer, or would you choose the approach used by the United States? That might be a subject for a most interesting Gallup poll.

## No Fun?

To say Singapore is no fun is unfair. To say that it will be clean fun is entirely justifiable. The reasons no gum wrappers end up on the street are the $10,000 fine for selling gum and an automatic fine of about $250 for littering. But don't worry too much as a foreigner. The Singaporeans are so friendly and concerned about other people that when an obvious tourist dropped paper on the street, I saw a local person quickly pick it up and dispose of it properly so the foreigner would not be fined.

132

# SINGAPORE
## Swiss Twin and Key to the Pacific Rim

One of the newest forms of clean fun in Singapore is Penguin Parade, Singapore's answer to Sea World. Among other things, it contains one hundred penguins of various species waddling among a landscape of rocks, cliffs, nesting alcoves, and burrows that would impress even America's TV zoologist, Jack Hanna! The Penguin Parade is just one of the exhibits at Jurong Bird Haven. If you are like me, you might question whether a day at a bird park could be very exciting. After trying it, my recommendation is not to miss Jurong Bird Haven. It is a fascinating, environmentally advanced national park with more than five thousand birds of more than 450 species. And in Singapore, even the bird cages are clean! I don't know how they do it.

## Democracy or Authoritacracy?

Singapore's Lee Kuan Yew is one of the most amazing leaders the modern world has produced. Former President Richard Nixon, in his book *1999*, described leaders he has known during more than forty years of global relationships. None, Mr. Nixon says, has impressed him more than Singapore's leader, Mr. Lee. When Nelson Mandela met with Lee Kuan Yew in 1993, a scheduled one-hour appointment was extended to an entire day. Mr. Mandela reportedly was deeply impressed with Mr. Lee's views about values and discipline as the keys to success for a nation.

Mr. Lee is an urban planner by education. His training shines through in every part of the city in areas as disparate as the airport and the education system. His approach to government-influenced capitalism is well illustrated by a recent government decision. After careful analysis, the government concluded that an increasing number of lawyers in a society serves to decrease the economic growth of the country. As an example of the planned approach to economic development, the government has cut the number of lawyers to be produced by law schools in order to bring the balance to a number by the year 2000 that will discourage litigation and encourage economic activity.

Planning is a key to Singapore's efficiency. The freeways are not crowded. Partly that is due to excellence in design. More importantly, the government does not issue more permits to use the freeways than they can safely and swiftly accommodate. And nearly as many flowers are blooming along the streets as you would find at an international floral festival.

Everything that should not be done carries a fine. There is a fine for not flushing toilets. (That is one of the reasons Changi toilets do not smell bad.) There is a fine for littering. There is a fine for trafficking in chewing gum but not for chewing it. I have mentioned this to some people who were shocked, asking why anyone would object to selling chewing gum. That, some have said, is un-American. If you are one of those persons, check out Disney World and increasingly most airports. You will not find gum sold at Disney World.

In general, if you like Disney World, you will like Singapore. They both have prohibitions against chewing gum, long hair, litter, violence, and many other forms of antisocial or deviant behavior. Singapore is an entire country run with the efficiency methods of a Disney World.

At a recent educators conference of the American Marketing Association I presented a paper on economic development and mentioned Singapore favorably. One of the professors in the audience commented during the question and answer period, "You neglected to tell people that Singapore is a police state." I asked him, "Have you ever been to Singapore?" His answer was no but that he knew people who had been there. Since this was a group of international professors, I asked the audience who among them had been to Singapore. In the audience, about a third of the hands went up. I asked them, "Would you consider Singapore a police state?"

Uniformly, the answer was no; it is one of the best countries in the world. In my trips to Singapore, I have rarely seen police. Singapore has lots of rules—but I doubt that anyone could examine any one of the rules and not agree that people are better off when they obey the rules. And that is precisely what nearly everyone in

Singapore does. They obey the rules. Do they obey the rules because they believe that justice will be swift and certain? Or do they obey the rules because they believe the rules will lead to a better quality of life for themselves and the nation?

I cannot answer that question. But two things are certain. People obey the rules and people are prosperous in Singapore.

In America, we are presented with an assumption throughout life that democracy is better than authoritacracy. Perhaps we believe in democracy on religious grounds, or perhaps we believe in it because we have been taught in school that we should believe in democracy, or perhaps we just believe in democracy because most other people say it is best.

Such assumptions are more philosophical than empirical. Economies such as Singapore's, Korea's, and others' provide empirical evidence that authoritacracies intertwined with democracy can be very effective in providing prosperity for a nation's people. The confrontation between democracy and authoritacracy raises a fascinating question. Does a wise and benevolent dictator perhaps provide a better form of government than an ignorant and selfish person elected by the democratic process?

## *Survival, Security, and Success*

Singapore is highly successful. Most of its success has to be credited to its value system, not to an abundance of natural resources. In that and other ways, it is much like Switzerland.

Singapore is also like Switzerland in its cultural diversity and acceptance. In Singapore are found people of Chinese, Malay, Indian, British, and other cultures. Many languages are spoken in the home. All the world's great religions are well represented. At business luncheons to which I have been invited, several serving tables are evident. Each one serves the food relevant to various religions present: Muslim, Kosher, Hindu, and so forth. It is a great experience for a visitor to be able to sample some of each, but it also caused me to wonder whether the typical American businessperson has enough sensitivity to provide guests with vegetarian, Kosher, or whatever may be the appropriate food.

Some observers attribute the Japanese economic success to cultural homogeneity. That is easily refuted by visiting Singapore, where cultural diversity is the rule. The cultural contributions of each ethnic group are celebrated in schools, the media, and Singapore's major museum, Pioneers of Singapore. In brilliant and creative exhibits, the pioneers of Singapore are portrayed.

The Pioneers represent people from all walks of life and ethnic groups, those famous as well as those unnamed, all of whom had a share in laying the foundations of Singapore as a shipping and trading center in the Orient. The museum is typical of the government's efforts to stimulate the interest of young and old in the Singaporean heritage. Such efforts are built upon the premise of Lee Kuan Yew: "To understand the present and anticipate the future, one must know enough of the past to have a sense of the history of a people."

As an example of the ability to be pragmatic about values, the government changed the official languages to fit the need to be prosperous instead of lamenting the ability to be prosperous. By cultural heritage, many people in Singapore speak Cantonese, Malay, Hindi, or other languages. But the government decided that the country would be most prosperous if everyone would learn English—the global language of business—and Mandarin—the language of Beijing, rather than Cantonese, the language of Hong Kong. Those languages have been adopted as the official languages of the country and are taught in schools.

Why those languages? Certainly not because they are the languages people learned in the past. No, because if you live in Singapore, English and Mandarin are the languages you need to be prosperous in the future.

We can learn from the Singaporeans even in the matter of language. Many immigrants have come to the United States from around the world. The ones who prosper are usually the ones who learn the language needed to prosper in business today and tomorrow. And the sooner and better they learn the most useful language, the more likely they are to prosper. That process does not minimize the desirability of maintaining facility with diverse languages nor appreciation of cultural heritage from the past, but it does recognize the need to adapt to the future instead of holding on to a fading past.

What can we learn from Singapore? Perhaps the most useful lesson is about values and how a country, a corporation, a family, or an individual can benefit from understanding what values they should have in order to live the lifestyle they desire. Lee Kuan Yew provided a view almost as important to understanding Singapore as the Preamble is to the American Constitution.

Mr. Lee said it this way: "Singapore is an immigrant society. Our values are those which assure survival, security, and success."

In most any other country of the world, most any person can learn some important lessons from Singapore. That's the way I see it . . . from the edge.

137

# 11

# SOUTH AFRICA
*Hong Kong of Africa?*

**When asked to name the most beautiful country** in the world, world travelers often name New Zealand with its combination of beaches, mountains, and agricultural areas. I have not been to New Zealand, but I have been to South Africa. South Africa is my choice as the most beautiful country in the world with its incredibly complex environment that ranges from subtropic deserts to snow-covered (occasionally) mountains, jungle forests, the windswept *highveld* plateau area, modern cities, as well as ancient Dutch and French homes. In the south of South Africa, the coast of the Cape Province separating the Atlantic and Indian oceans has few rivals for drama and beauty, even when compared with the French Riviera or the Pacific Coast of the United States.

138

Kids are the same around the world

## *The Real South Africa*

South Africa contains some of the most modern cities and infrastructure in the world. Its railroads, airlines, ports and highways, utilities, manufacturers, and mines are as efficient and sophisticated as any in the world. You can drink the water without fear anyplace in the country. You can stay in hotels such as Southern or Proteus that rival Marriott for service. You can stay in City Lodge hotels that rival Red Roof Inns for economy and cleanliness. You can receive treatment in hospitals so advanced that the Mayo Clinic and major U.S. medical schools depend on them for new technology and personnel.

Yet, just a few kilometers from the most modern cities in the world, you can be transported in time to other cultures containing

A customer examines merchandise on the ground in an informal Soweto market

the throbbing, raw energy of ethnic groups who have changed very little for thousands of years. In a matter of minutes, a plane can whisk you into the midst of a safari where you can watch elephants, lions, giraffe, and many other animals live and die by the law of nature pretty much as they have been doing for centuries. You can walk from one area of Durban to another and be transported from the last vestiges of the British colonial empire to curry-scented markets that are bustling with accents and incense in a trading fervor reminiscent of New Delhi or Calcutta.

I have taught in South African universities for more than a decade as well as served on Ohio State's Presidential Advisory Committee on South Africa, which led Ohio State to be one of the first universities to disinvest as a protest against apartheid. I have toured schools in South Africa, both integrated and segregated, that rank among the best and the worst in the world.

I have shopped in hypermarkets that are larger and more modern than any retail facilities in Europe or North America. I have also shopped at small *spaza* shops, black-owned food retailers in the informal sector of the economy that represent the new entrepreneurs of South Africa. I have ridden in black-owned taxis, which have almost eliminated the government-owned bus system, and which now employ more workers than all the gold mines in South Africa, and have visited *sheebeens*, black-owned nightclubs. I have jogged through black townships, met with a village witch doctor, watched workers blast and pick gold while I was two miles under the surface of the earth, eaten meals with both mine workers and managing directors, and created friendships that in all the world are among some of my best and longest lasting. Other than the United States, South Africa is the country I know and love best.

## A Difficult Nonpolitical View

As a reader, you might expect me to talk mostly about the civil strife, funerals, violence, and political problems of South Africa. That is what most people see most of the time in the newspapers. But in this chapter, I intend to speak very little about the political issues of South Africa for two reasons. First, those are the things you can already read about in newspapers. Unfortunately, they are usually the only things you can read about in newspapers.

I have never seen a newspaper article or a TV news program showing normal life in Soweto, with hundreds of thousands of modest homes that look very much like the millions of similar homes built in America in the late 1940s and early 1950s. I have never seen an article explaining the very great love for family and God that is expressed in so many ways by the majority of both black and nonblack segments of the South African population. I have never seen articles about the love of nature and the environment that is so intense among most South Africans that it would be the envy of the Sierra Club.

# SOUTH AFRICA
## *Hong Kong of Africa?*

I have never seen pictures of the many modern stores, banks, and other businesses that learned years ago that it is not black or white but green that is the relevant color for business. The press rarely talks about the millions of workers who endure violence and many other risks and hardships to commute from the townships to their jobs. I have never seen stories about the prosperous black leaders who live in beautiful new homes with a Mercedes in the garage in the upscale areas of Soweto, and never have I seen stories about the prosperous black families who have lived in officially white suburbia for the past decade—in about the same proportions of the black families who live in officially integrated suburbia of the United States. Yet, this is the real South Africa.

The second reason I am avoiding writing about the political issues of South Africa is that doing so misses the real South Africa— the people, the places, and the process of what is happening throughout Southern Africa. Frankly, also, by the time I write about the political situation in South Africa, it will have changed. I have chosen to write about what will still exist in South Africa five, ten, or fifty years from now. Storm clouds hover over South Africa concerning political control but the people and their values, the physical resources, and most of the infrastructure will continue. Those are the elements of the real South Africa.

I have studied South Africa as intensively as any country in the world. I have published academic papers about the country and discussed issues with government officials and business executives, African National Congress leaders, and others, as well as South African and American media. I have listened intently to the views of campus leaders in the United States, South Africa, and other countries. I can tell you with great conviction that the people who say they know what will happen politically in South Africa in the future are people who have never been to South Africa and who probably know very little about the country. The most knowledgeable analysts of South Africa build scenarios, not forecasts.

## *The New South Africa*

The new South Africa is much like areas of the United States such as Alabama, Mississippi, or Georgia. Those former bastions of segregation and discrimination now contain large areas of opportunity for the predominantly black citizens. Although previously disenfranchised most in those areas, some black friends tell me that cities such as Atlanta and Birmingham offer more opportunities than northern cities that were officially integrated much earlier.

Groups of the population believe in violence to promote their views. Some of the groups reflect black leadership—such as the Pan African Congress—who believe whites should be eliminated from the future of South Africa. Some of the groups represent the right wing elements of white Afrikaner culture—the first settlers in the area arising from the Dutch culture—who believe that their ancient family lands should be protected from transfer to black ownership. Other very serious threats to the new South Africa—and the source of most of the fatalities to date—derive from historic ethnic conflict, especially between the Zulu and the Xhosa ethnic groups. The problems of South Africa are fundamentally the same as those in Ireland, Bosnia, or Lebanon.

I have spent many hours talking to individuals from all of those groups. They do not know how the new South Africa will handle these conflicts. Nor does anyone else. And one of the lessons that we must learn in the United States is that we have the potential for many of the same problems.

But there is a new South Africa. It is forming politically with historic votes and elections. Economically, however, it began when former President George Bush lifted sanctions against South Africa in 1991. I was in South Africa on that historic day that started South Africa on a new role as trading partner and provisioner for much of Africa. On that day, I visited a large research institution near Johannesburg. Its leaders had hoisted an American flag to welcome me and to symbolize the new era. As I drove toward the stars and stripes, I was glad that my country once again could support

South Africa's drive to a new future. I am saddened today, however, when I learn that some cities and others refuse to change laws put on the books during the sanctions era, because it serves a local competitor's interest to keep foreign competition from bidding on local projects. Late in 1993 Nelson Mandela called for an end to these sanctions, and soon, I hope, that will happen.

Even during sanctions, many relationships existed between South Africa and other African nations. I met businesspeople who traveled, without their South African passport, to other African countries arranging sales of railroad equipment, wine, food, computer equipment, and many other products and services. But travel generally was clandestine, with official denials and condemnation of South Africa in the press, even though as individuals, South Africans and leaders of other countries often gathered at night as friends over a bottle of South African wine.

The new South Africa can now trade openly with other countries. South African Airways used to fly around Africa at great expense of time and fuel to get to Europe because the rest of Africa barred it from flying over its space. Now South African Airways flies from Johannesburg to Cairo and is emerging as the primary carrier for all of Africa. The same is true for railways, electricity, trucking, and many other areas of technology.

Some relationships are still strained but most are opening up, both with the rest of Africa and with the rest of the world. South Africa is now a country with a first-world economy and infrastructure in the midst of the fast-growing markets of a third-world country and neighbor to many more fast-growing third-world markets.

## *Understanding Third-World Perceptions*

Understanding the reaction of third-world consumers to first-world promotions can be illustrated by a conversation I witnessed between Justice, a twenty-three-year-old groundskeeper and his employer. Justice has a reasonably good education compared to many people in Africa, about the equivalent of a sophomore in a U.S. high school. He was bothered by something he had heard but could not believe, namely that the world was round.

As is often the case, Justice went to his employer to ask if that could be true. His employer, a professor friend of mine, explained that indeed the world is round. He went to great efforts to demonstrate with a basketball and oranges how this works. Justice was so impressed, he brought a roomful of his friends to hear the entire explanation again.

My professor friend, who teaches marketing, was pleased with the contribution to knowledge he thought he had made. A few days later Justice talked to him again and said he had thought about it a lot, and he and his friends had decided that the professor was wrong—the earth really is flat. Although only members of the Flat Earth Society might fail to find this anecdote amusing, advertising and marketing people must communicate with third-world consumers who process information about new products and how to use them with as much skepticism as Justice when confronted with the unbelievable claim that the earth is round.

## First-World Opportunities

South Africa is a country that now can offer great opportunities for many first-world firms. That is why, as this is being written, firms such as Hyatt Hotels are reportedly looking for locations and Holiday Inn is already well represented. Microsoft has announced its interest in investing in South Africa, as have many lesser known computer and software firms.

Johannesburg is a city that looks and functions pretty much like Houston, Columbus, or other modern American cities. Favorite TV programs are often the same as in the United States, including "L.A. Law," "60 Minutes," and "Rescue 911." Johannesburg (including nearby Soweto) is the largest city in this country of 37 million people, many of whom have an exceptionally high standard of living and industrial base. Considerable disparity exists in income among the four major population groups, but white consumers have among the highest in the world and even the masses of predominantly black consumers have per capita incomes several times the average of the rest of Africa.

Johannesburg is the home of the most modern and largest hypermarket in the world, Pick-n-Pay in Boxburg. This store averages more than R 1 million a day and hit a record of R 2.6 million (equivalent to about 1 million U.S. dollars) in a single day. It sets a standard in service, merchandising, and the use of store brands that Kroger or Safeway might want to emulate. It is one of the firms we describe in detail in *Contemporary Cases in Consumer Behavior*.

NCR equipment dominates 116 checkout lanes at the world's largest hypermarket. On Saturday mornings, all lines are packed with consumers of all colors and income levels. You will see store brands in Pick-n-Pay that I believe no other supermarket in the world can rival in quality of design and execution, with the possible exception of Loblaws in Canada.

A multibillion-dollar firm such as Pick-n-Pay is an attractive distributor, however, for many branded products of firms such as Johnson and Johnson and other U.S. companies. During the sanctions era, many people probably wondered why firms such as Johnson and Johnson stayed in South Africa. Yet if you understand the fertility rates of Africa and the commitment that a firm with the integrity of Johnson and Johnson has to all people, especially babies, you can understand why it keeps its commitment not only to South Africa but to the mothers and their babies throughout the entire continent.

I talked with the produce manager of a Pick-n-Pay store and was impressed with his knowledge about all aspects of the organization, including margins, turnovers, and overall profit trends throughout the chain. I know many Americans believe that American managers are better qualified than those in other parts of the world. I could not help but doubt, however, that I could find a similar high level of marketing knowledge among most of the personnel in American supermarkets. Do you find it interesting that it is necessary to travel to Africa to find one of the best managed retailers in the world, one that most American retailers could benefit greatly by studying?

Pizza Hut and Kentucky Fried Chicken are big in South Africa. I learned that McDonald's is looking for sites now, and I couldn't help but wonder which other American food chains would soon be there. Wendy's would be a good bet in some of the upscale shopping centers if it could overcome the cultural value that white consumers will not eat any food without a fork. I also think that White Castle or Burger King might find a new gold mine in South Africa by locating in a township such as Soweto with a population of several million people, many of whom live in middle-class homes, have rapidly rising incomes, and are aware of most American firms through watching "Sanford and Son" or other favorite programs dubbed on television in Xhosa, Zulu, or Sotho.

The greatest opportunity for American exporters may be among the many computer and software firms and the numerous and sophisticated manufacturing and transportation firms. Computer firms such as Legent and Symix are naturals for computer-oriented South Africa. Security is a major problem among South Africa's modern retail malls, a natural outlet for the security systems of a firm such as Checkpoint.

TransNet, the operator of South Africa's airlines, railways, ports, and trucking could use the railroad components of Harmon Industries, Buckeye Steel Castings, or many other American firms. It might also be a market for the services of the many logistics management and distribution firms that have exploded in size and importance in recent years. Even GE's industrial diamond division might provide technology to the natural diamond industry that is so much a part of South Africa's economy.

South Africa's largest research organization, Mintek, is possibly the most sophisticated mining, metallurgical, and chemical engineering organization in the world. It is already a big user of Chemical Abstract's services and is a logical candidate for services or strategic alliances with Battelle, Online Computer Library Center (OCLC), and other technology organizations.

Many North American (as well as European and Asian) firms will find many reasons to travel to South Africa in an effort to open up export markets. They will even find it easy to travel there on the new nonstop flights of South African Airways, consistently voted by international travelers as the best African airline, or perhaps on some of the new flights Delta and other American airlines are readying for South Africa. But as attractive as South Africa may be for many North American export-oriented firms, there is an even bigger attraction to South Africa.

## *Visit the Harbor, Stay in a Prison*

To some degree, South Africa occupies a role analogous to Singapore, with Durban and Cape Town being key ports in what is emerging as another major regional economic area. Professor Steve Burgess of the University of Witswatersrand in Johannesburg calls this trading community the Indian Ocean Rim, and it is a fast growing area of the Southern Hemisphere.

The ports of South Africa are among the most modern and efficient in the world. One of the premier South African ports is in Cape Town. The port services more than a hundred ships daily and thus brings jobs and business to the surrounding area. But just as importantly, the port functions as one of the most popular tourist attractions in the southern part of South Africa. Table Mountain serves as the perfect backdrop for a myriad of shops, restaurants, markets, and special events. The excitement of trade occurring at the port is carried up to the shores of the harbor and spreads through the retail shops.

If you do visit the area, be sure to stay at the Breakwater Lodge for a unique experience. The building, which overlooks the harbor, used to be a prison but was converted to a hotel. After extensive remodeling, it now also houses Cape Town's graduate busi-

South Africa's ports are its gateways to the rest of Africa

ness school. I'm sure you're snickering at this. Most business students would agree that a prison would be an appropriate place for most business professors to spend their days.

## *Base for Intermarket Segmentation*

South Africa's own markets provide only one of the attractions for firms in many countries. The other attraction is that South Africa is the nucleus for trade and technology throughout southern Africa. For decades China has been a country whose masses of laborers and consumers were generally accessed through Hong Kong. I believe there is a high probability that South Africa will play much the same financial, technical, and logistical role for the rest of Africa, especially southern Africa.

149

South Africa has engaged in a great deal of trade and technology with other African nations that for political reasons officially denied such relationships in the past. Now many black African nations have recognized South Africa, and a steady stream of political and economic relationships is opening up between South Africa and countries such as Zaire, Ivory Coast, Kenya, Zimbabwe, and others. The railways of a number of African nations, already extending beyond the border states, are operated to a large extent by South Africa's Transnet. South Africa may become the Hong Kong of Africa—a gateway to the rest of the continent.

South Africa is such an efficient producer of foodstuffs (especially fresh produce), clothing, shoes, and other essentials that it is likely to have a booming trade with countries in Africa, Europe, and the Middle East. U.S. firms that supply products or services for those industries will find attractive markets in South Africa. Perhaps some American firms also will find the high-technology base and the low labor costs an attractive inducement to establish manufacturing facilities to sell in Asia, Europe, and the Middle East, even though Mexico is the more obvious choice for manufacturing products destined for North America.

The marketing concept relevant to understanding how to use South Africa as a conduit to all of Africa is called intermarket segmentation. (If you really think this topic might be useful to your firm, you might want to read an entire chapter on the subject that I wrote in another book with Professor Salah Hassan called *Global Marketing: Perspectives and Cases*, published by Harcourt Brace Jovanovich, 1994.)

For example, the market for electric turbines is not large in most any specific African country but when the amount of electrification that is occurring throughout the African continent is considered, the market is enormous. The entire market could be very important for a firm such as General Electric or Emerson Electric. But how can such a firm access each country?

The answer is on an intersegment basis. That is, a GE or Emerson sells to the same type of buyer in the same manner in all of

150

the countries. To do so, the exporter will probably need a distributor and technical service support system that understands the languages, exchange and payment problems, and culture of the widely varying nations. In all probability, the best place in Africa to find that distributor or base its own subsidiary will be South Africa. Thus, the trend toward intermarket segmentation provides one more reason to think of South Africa as the Hong Kong of Africa.

## Respect for Nature

The world is losing much of the past. This is true of the rain forests of Brazil, the aboriginals of Australia, and now much of the savanna and bush wildlife of Africa. In South Africa, much of the past is still preserved with a great sense of conservation and respect for the environment.

As an illustration, Nedbank, which is one of South Africa's leading banks and in some ways one of the leading banks of the world, bases much of its promotional material on support of the World Wildlife Fund. From adverts (as the rest of the world calls advertisements) that feature conservation themes, to panda-covered neckties as promotional gifts, to checks that display beautiful pictures of wild animals, to VISA cards that provide donations to the World Wildlife Fund, Nedbank has successfully promoted itself to its target customers using the conservation theme. I do not think that approach would be as effective in the United States because, except for a minority of consumers, we are rather backward in sensitivity to the environment.

But in South Africa, respect for nature by the majority of people is as natural as the sunrise. Perhaps that is one of the lessons Americans can learn from understanding Africa better.

## The Last Safari

If you have never taken an African safari, I recommend you do so as soon as possible. If you have already taken one in Kenya, South Af-

Nedbank is an innovative bank with a social conscience

rica, or some other country, consider taking it again. It could be your last safari. Poachers, cattle farmers, and drought are taking their toll on much of Africa. Most of the problems have been held back in South Africa, but one can only guess when even South Africa will give way to the "progress" of cattle farming.

The game lodges of South Africa today are unexcelled for availability of game, ease of transportation, and comfort for guests. The service is excellent, the scenery is breathtaking, and the prices currently are like buying designer clothes in Filene's bargain basement.

Most likely your travel agent will recommend Kruger National Park or one of the private game reserves near Kruger. The largest and best known is Sabi Sabi, and it is excellent. There are many others, and I have never heard a guest report anything other than good food, clean facilities, friendly and competent staff, and plentiful game.

My own favorite is *Ngala*, which in the local language means *lion*, and we saw lots of them. It is an incredible experience to have three young lions wake up on a sunny afternoon and amble over to rub against the knobby tires of your Land Rover. It is amazing to see a mother giraffe instructing and correcting a wobbly baby. We even saw one mother giraffe baby-sitting another's as well as her own while the other mother went out to scout some nearby trees.

Kruger National Park is about one-third the size of the state of Ohio, with many roads and camps of comfortable rondolas. These round huts may have thatched roofs, but they are air-conditioned in the summer and come complete with hot water bottles in the beds in the winter. They are rustic and luxurious at the same time. Kruger and the nearby private facilities are easily accessible by commuter aircraft from Johannesburg, or you can rent a car and drive the five or six hours from Johannesburg.

Be sure you arrive at Kruger before nightfall, because all gates are closed at dusk for a good reason. The people are all carefully secured in the campsites by dusk. The campsites have tall, heavy fences around the compound to keep out the wild animals. Kruger Park is a flip-flop environment in which the people are secondary and the wild animals are in charge. Visitors are locked inside for the night, allowing the animals to walk around the compound and stare at the humans. Admittedly, having wild animals stare at you is better than being eaten by them!

## Cry Freedom!

The year 1992 saw the abolition of every law in South Africa that promoted apartheid, something many people around the world have wished and worked for. But the abolition of apartheid does not bring liberation to the oppressed to any greater extent than the Emancipation Proclamation brought freedom to Americans of African descent. Nor does the progress we have witnessed in South Africa mean the end of racism any more than the enactment of civil

153

rights laws ended racism in America. Elimination of apartheid did not eliminate the great discrepancy between the "haves" and the "have nots" of this or any country. To be painfully analytical about the situation, one could conclude that economic conditions may be improved very little if at all by the new democracy in which all citizens are permitted to participate. More likely, the average person will be worse off economically. That sometimes is the price of freedom.

The future of South Africa is based not on political freedom, as important as that is; the future is based on economic freedom. South Africa has created a standard of living even among its poorest consumers that is the envy of the rest of Africa. Even during the era of apartheid, thousands of citizens of other countries tried to immigrate to South Africa because of its economic opportunity.

Today South Africa's borders are as much the target of illegal immigrants as are America's and for pretty much the same reasons. Maintaining and increasing the standard of living in South Africa will depend not only on its ability to achieve political stability in the future but also on its role in economic trade, some of which will be with American firms. If the progress continues, the combination of trade, technology, affluence, and multicultural diversity may truly create in the new post-apartheid South Africa a Hong Kong of Africa.

That's the way I see it . . . from the edge.

# 12

# WHAT IS THE FASTEST GROWING ECONOMY IN THE WORLD?

**If you were asked to name the fastest** growing economy in the world, how would you respond? Japan? Korea? Perhaps the economic miracle of the Orient, Singapore? If those were among your answers, you guessed wrong.

I'll give you a clue. Where is the only place in the world (to the best of my knowledge) that you can stand in one spot and be in or touch the boundaries of four nations?

You were right if you named tiny, landlocked Botswana in the heart of southern Africa. According to the World Bank, Botswana was the world's best in gross national product per capita growth in the 1965–1989 period. Its 8.5 percent average annual per capita growth since independence is even more impressive considering the population grew annually at an average of 3.5 percent.

Art is one contributor to this thriving economy

## *A Shining Example*

Globally oriented firms might find good reasons to visit Botswana as a market or source for U.S.-produced goods and services. My wife and I visited Botswana to discover why this growing but still poor country has experienced such economic success when many of its neighbors are struggling for economic survival.

In addition to the world's fastest per capita gross national product growth, Botswana holds the world's largest value share of diamond sales. Rather than spend the proceeds immediately, Botswana invests its capital in Swiss banks and uses the investment income to build infrastructure—schools, hospitals, and roads. The way Botswana has handled its most important natural resource should be a shining example for the rest of the developing countries.

The market-oriented government has created partnerships with foreign firms such as AMAX, British Petroleum, Anglo-American, and AECI, assuring continued development of Botswana's excellent mineral resources. The development of those natural resources might provide opportunities for resource firms as diverse as Ashland Chemical or mining manufacturer Dresser Industries. Even heavy equipment distributors such as W. W. Williams may find opportunities in African countries such as Botswana.

Stable government and sound economic practices led to Botswana's very healthy balance of payments position. The country is the recipient of investments by numerous global firms such as Heinz, Colgate-Palmolive, Lonrho, and Metal Box and a host of South African firms in recent years. They think of Botswana as a great place to locate their operations to serve other parts of Africa. While South Africa might be considered the ideal location for a company's African headquarters in terms of logistics and technology, it does not possess the political stability of Botswana—at least not at this time.

## *Where on Earth?*

Perhaps you are still puzzled by the identity of the other three countries in the geography clue I gave you in the first paragraph. The other three countries are Namibia, Zambia, and Zimbabwe. On a spot near Kasane, all four countries converge. If nothing else, that tidbit of information will make a great brainteaser at your next dinner party.

Two dominating geographic factors can be found in Botswana: the Kalahari Desert and the Okavango Swamps. The Kalahari is responsible for the country's chronic water shortages. It is a fascinating combination of beauty and danger that sustains life one moment and kills it the next. While nomadic tribes do roam the area, at first glance much of the desert seems barren, which in itself is another form of serene beauty. The swamps are alive with dangerous wildlife, such as monstrous crocodiles, and hundreds of varieties of graceful and colorful birds.

## *Under the Baobab Tree*

Development of amenities in the Okavango Swamps and the Chobe National Park could lead to Botswana's recognition as one of the world's leading tourist attractions. Nearby Victoria Falls is already recognized as one of the seven natural wonders of the world, easily accessible by air from Harare or Johannesburg. If you do visit the falls, keep in mind that you will get wet—we caught on to that fact quickly when we saw all the raincoat rental booths.

My wife and I were fortunate enough to stay in Mowana Safari Lodge. Mowana means "Place of the Baobab" tree. It is a brand new, truly first-class lodge built around a massive baobab tree. Located on the banks of the Chobe River, which empties into the Zambezi River, Mowana is only one of the many safari lodges that offer excellent food, friendly and efficient service, and some of the most spectacular contacts with nature to be found in the world.

One of the advantages of a lodge such as Mowana is that it provides both overland safaris (in adjacent Chobe National Park) by four-wheel-drive vehicles and amazing overwater safaris by boat on the Chobe River. Few sights are as breathtaking as thousands of elephants streaming down from the hills each evening to romp, spray, and drink from the banks of the Chobe River. Huge crocodiles as well as thousands of massive hippos sun on the banks. It is best, however, not to have the boat too close to the crocodiles when they are hungry or on top of the hippos when they come up for air!

Lions, giraffe, warthogs, baboons and monkeys, wildebeest, and antelope of every description—they are all abundant and accessible in Botswana. When driving from one village to the next you would see elephants cross the road, just as we are accustomed to seeing rabbits and squirrels. However, the results would be different if you hit the elephant rather than the bunny.

## *Where Is Detroit?*

For a researcher on global marketing, one of the most interesting and at the same time depressing sights is the hustle and bustle of vehicles of all types. Most are owned by firms doing business in the active tourism, mining, and distribution industries of Botswana.

The depressing fact for an American business professor is that not one of the vehicles I saw was from the United States. There are four-wheel drives by Isuzu, Nissan, and Toyota everywhere in Africa—but I saw not one Jeep. We may know how to make good vehicles in Detroit (and in Toledo, for Jeeps), but we certainly don't market them well.

It is popular today to be a Japan basher and complain about the lack of a level playing field in Japan as the cause of the decline of American auto firms. I am more concerned about the reasons American firms are not competitive against Japanese firms where they *do* play on a level, although rugged, playing field. Botswana and other African countries provide such a turf.

## Why?

Why is Botswana thriving? Around a campfire one night I asked some young men to tell me about their country compared to other African countries. They told me about violence, corruption, and lack of discipline in neighboring countries. The young men had the equivalent of a junior high education but spoke English well. They were more than eager to tell me about their country and how they saw the future.

One of the young men explained why some countries prosper and others do not and why some African countries are more violent than others. "It is a result of their ideology," he explained. My wife then asked them where they thought people got their ideology. "From parents," he answered.

We could not help but wonder if such profundity would be found among junior high students in the United States—or even among most adults. His answer was not one that he had learned from a book. It was not one he had heard on television. It was one that came from his heart—where his parents had placed it with their upbringing. Regardless of its origin, his answer was right.

159

The two countries with the highest gross domestic product in the world are Switzerland and Japan, and they have almost no natural resources. Yet countries with enormous natural resources, such as Russia, Brazil, and Nigeria, are making little economic progress.

It is not natural resources that cause nations or individuals to prosper, even though countries such as Botswana and the United States are fortunate to have them. The ultimate cause of prosperity is a nation's values. You have read about this topic in other chapters. I believe our young friend in Botswana was right when he explained why one country is good and another is bad: "It is one's ideology."

It is difficult to hear thoughts that profound without thinking of the lessons that might help my own country. In the United States, we talk glibly about American values and the latest phrase, "family values." Yet how often have you heard someone describe them? Not often, because it is not an easy thing to do. In my textbook with Professors James Engel and Paul Miniard (*Consumer Behavior*, Harcourt Brace Jovanovich, 1993), I wrote a chapter on culture. There I describe some of the values that are most commonly accepted in the United States, but even this is not an attempt to define which values *should* be accepted.

What if some of the values that constitute our ideology in the United States are the wrong ones for stability, survival, and success in the future? What mechanisms do we have for changing them? We pride ourselves in the United States on our status as an immigrant nation. The United States was founded by immigrants from diverse backgrounds who were able to agree, more or less, on a common ideology. It was an ideology that has been enriched by additions from many immigrants since the founding of the country.

But what if a prospective immigrant does not share that ideology or core of values? Should that person still be allowed to enter and become a citizen of the United States? What if a person has contributed to the decline of his or her own nation by having bad values relating to crime, violence, drugs, disease, education, or creating and raising children? Should that person still be allowed to immigrate to the United States? If people prove by their behavior that they do not have values that contribute to the success of the nation, should they be deported? Should persons who have ruined their own country by overpopulation or crime or lack of discipline in obtaining an education be permitted to immigrate to America and contribute to its decline as well?

The young man in the middle of Africa caused me to do a lot of thinking about the ideology of my own country on that quiet night around the campfire in Botswana. I hope you are also thinking about those same questions and their answers. I believe they are the questions that lead to the ultimate answers about the causes of success, not only for countries, but for corporations and other institutions as well as for families and individuals.

## The Tenth Century

Perhaps the richest experience of all was the opportunity to visit two traditional villages. One was a Setswana village, the other a Khoisan village. Most areas of Africa have a great deal of contact with modern society, but we went out of our way to find villages that had almost no contact with contemporary economies. In most ways, they had changed little from what could have been observed in the tenth century.

Most of the children had never seen a white woman—let alone someone with blonde hair. It was a little scary for them! They wanted nothing to do with the idea of my wife picking them up and carrying them. She could have been an alien from Mars landing in the middle of Montana and probably caused no more fear than she did in this little village of Botswana. In comparison, I was accepted like a king.

In the traditional Setswana village, we found almost no evidence of contact with the twentieth century, except for one small storage building with a corrugated metal roof. All other buildings were made of mud with thatched roofs. There was no running

Home or art? A Setswana hut decorated with clay paintings

water, no electricity, no other evidences of the industrial world. The homes were painted brightly, however, with pictures of elephants and lions made of colors gathered from the soil. Their beauty and feeling rivaled the paintings of Miró, Calder, or Lichtenstein.

The people of the village had not a single one of the conveniences we take for granted in the United States, except for a box of Johnson and Johnson baby powder that one young mother proudly showed us. Yet they seemed very happy.

The village residents arise each morning without the benefit of an alarm clock or Bryant Gumble. They tend crops and cattle, hunt, and live their lives without faxes or cellular phones. They go to sleep without the benefit of sedatives or laxatives. Their average longevity is about what it was in the United States a hundred years ago, and their average gross domestic product in these traditional villages is nearly nonexistent. But they appear to live very well.

162

They do have reasons for plenty of stress. Elephants trampling your crops and lions eating your cattle are pretty stressful events. I saw a hospital about forty kilometers away from the village, where in rare instances a village resident might be taken, but the hospital had no mental illness wing.

As a professor, I presented an academic paper less than a month after visiting those villages. The topic of the paper and some of my other research focused on how to stimulate growth of GDP in developing countries. Yet the people I visited had no GDP and appeared to be very content with their lives. Some young men leave the village, of course, bound for cities, safari lodges, or the diamond mines from which they earn relatively high incomes. But if we professors figure out how to increase the GDP of the people in this village, if we bring them running water, electricity, and infant formula, and if we increase their average longevity by thirty or forty

years, will we have helped them? Is quality of life measured by external or internal conditions?

It is a moving experience to meet people who are not only from a different culture but in most ways from a different era. In Botswana, we found cities and resorts that had all the advantages of the twentieth century from airlines to air conditioners.

In the traditional villages, we also found people with none of the accoutrements of modern society. But they impressed us with their joy, friendliness, and a zest for life that surpassed what you observe among most people in the cities of America. They felt deeply satisfied with life even though the people of this traditional African village had no floors, no television, and almost no per capita GDP.

The naturalist with whom we worked to arrange the trip had visited the village eight months earlier and talked with the elders to ask if it would be acceptable to bring visitors to the village; but we were the first actually to visit. The first question asked of us by the villagers was, "What took you so long? We've been waiting for you." The last question asked of us was, "When will you come back to see us?"

Soon, we hope, were our unspoken words as we left Botswana, the world's fastest growing economy but also home of some of the world's poorest but richest people.

That's the way I see it . . . from the edge of the world!

# 13

# PERU

*A Study in Contrasts*

**¿Como Esta Usted?**

I hope your answer would be, "Muy bien, gracias, ¿y usted?"

If that was not your answer, I hope you would at least understand the question. It is the most common greeting and response you will encounter in Spanish and one I heard often during my visit to Peru.

When students or others ask me about how to prepare for the global economy, my answer always includes the advice to learn a foreign language. When asked which language is the best one to know, my answer is usually that it does not matter. Just studying any other language is important in developing the ability to function cross-culturally; but if pressed, I would have to say that the most important second language for most Americans is Spanish.

## *Why Spanish?*

Two reasons cause me to recommend Spanish. The first reason is that it is the second most common language in the United States (replacing German, which until recent decades was the most frequent second language). Knowing Spanish is therefore the most likely language to promote communication among Americans of different cultural backgrounds.

It always mystifies me how companies that employ large numbers of Spanish-speaking individuals can tolerate managers who never make the effort to learn some Spanish in order to facilitate better communication among all employees.

Service Master is a U.S. firm that employs large numbers of Latinos to provide cleaning services to hospitals and other institutions. It also employs large numbers of college-educated managers who usually do not understand Spanish. So Service Master, I'm told, encourages its managers to learn Spanish if they supervise numerous Spanish-speaking employees. With these and other policies that recognize the importance of individuals, it is not surprising that Service Master was noted by a financial publication as the most profitable company in the United States during the last decade. For the period 1980–1990, Service Master averaged 56 percent return on equity. I don't attribute that all to encouraging managers to learn Spanish, but Service Master does set a good example for other firms.

The second reason why Americans should study Spanish is because Latin American countries represent some of the best opportunities for global business relationships. Even at a time when the North American Free Trade Agreement is generating much opposition from labor and other groups, I believe that we should be thinking beyond NAFTA, toward a Community of the Americas, a regional economic organization that would be designed to compete with the European Community and include many of the countries of North, Central, and South America.

Thus, when I was asked to speak to the Congreso de Mercado in Lima, Peru, I could not turn down the invitation. The marketing conference brought together business and political representatives from many Latin American countries to discuss the topic of open markets—an increasing reality in many Latin American countries.

I always regret the poor quality of my own Spanish when in situations of this nature. Lima was no exception. I gave part of my speech in Spanish until someone finally suggested, "Speak English, please, it is easier to understand." Apparently, my good English was understood more readily than my bad Spanish. But I did receive good comments for trying. My informal Spanish did allow me to participate in conversations that otherwise would have been lost to me. I wish I had studied more in my high school Spanish classes!

I believe the same is true for businesspeople. Even if your knowledge of a foreign language is limited, people in the other culture usually appreciate your effort. In the case of Spanish, I had a few years of instruction, which at least allows me to read the newspapers. In most of the countries I travel, I don't have any formal instruction; but I believe it is always important to learn at least a few phrases that can be used when meeting new friends.

## The Latin American Economies

If most American businesspeople are aware of the opportunities in any Latin market, interest is probably focused on Mexico. That is appropriate, as you will read in chapter 15. But much more is south of the Mexican border. Latin American economies are growing and business leaders need to understand the realities of doing business in Latin America.

Peru might not be the first choice for most American firms to expand to Latin America. Peru's neighbor to the south, Chile, would probably be the best choice because of the recent strength of its economy. More than 7 percent of U.S. wine sales are now imported from Chile. Copper, which once represented almost all of Chile's exports, has been replaced by wine and many other products. Colombia, Argentina, Brazil, or some of the Central American countries might also be a better choice for a focus on global business opportunities.

But I visited Lima and was fascinated by the country. It is growing in population, as are all Latin American economies. It is plagued by inflation and other problems that affect most Latin American economies. Understanding Peru helps us understand many of the challenges of doing business in Latin America. Peru is a little more challenging than most, but focusing on Peru may even help us understand where the United States is headed if it does not come to grips with violence and the challenges of ethnic diversity.

## *A Country of Contrasts*

Peru is a country of contrasts. It is a country of quite a few wealthy people and many poor people. It is a blend of indigenous Indian culture and lots of Spanish infusion of culture. Peru includes some English immigrants and lots of Oriental immigrants, many of whom have become government and business leaders.

Contrasts abound in topography. It is a country about one-sixth the size of the United States and includes just as much variation—maybe more. The country has every kind of climate, a huge coastline, the Andes mountains, and near-desert areas in central and southern Peru, as well as the Selva, a huge area of lush, tropical forest so vast that much of it has hardly been explored.

Peru has excellent natural resources, including oil, copper, and vast amounts of timber. As you have read throughout this book, however, natural resources are not associated with the prosperity of a nation. Natural resources are often associated with poverty, and Peru is no exception.

Peru has about 25 million citizens and is growing at 3 percent a year, a rate many times faster than the United States. Peru has excellent schools and universities but many people who have never been to them. Competition to get into Peru's universities is intense.

People are moving from rural areas to cities in large numbers, a common problem of countries in Latin America and elsewhere. Some live in modern multistory apartment houses built by the government. Many end up living in *pueblos jovenes*, young towns composed of shanties and improvised sanitary and other facilities. They often are centers of unemployment, crime, and social problems.

The shanty villages are sharp contrasts to the bedroom suburbs of San Isidro, Miraflores, and others that have modern homes and pleasant gardens—often staffed with domestic servants who are readily available at about the equivalent of fifty U.S. dollars a month.

## Supermarkets and Inca-Cola

The contrasts continue everywhere. Modern commercial buildings stand in contrast to deteriorating buildings. Buildings with contemporary architecture provide a stark contrast to the old, historical buildings of central Lima.

The contrasts continue in the marketing of groceries. Although street vendors are omnipresent, Lima is also home of one of the finest supermarket chains. Operated by an oriental family that immigrated to Peru, the multiunit operation fascinated me. In the United States, outstanding supermarket operators would include Byerly's in Minnesota, Stew Leonard's in Connecticut, Buehler's in Ohio, and others. But I have not seen better promotions or better service in those outstanding operators than I did in Lima.

Throughout the store, people were cooking, baking, demonstrating, and promoting products. It was all I could do to keep from buying something at each place in the store. The store had an outstanding contest with the prize of a trip to Disney World. It was better conceived and executed than any I recall in United States supermarkets. One of the days I visited the store was Halloween. The

# PERU
*A Study in Contrasts*

Peru has plenty to offer consumers

supermarket was full of lines of costumed children, organized by area schools. Each child received a treat—and a favorable impression of the supermarket.

The store carried many brands from U.S. suppliers. One of the lessons to be learned by would-be exporters is to be wary of averages. The average income of Peru is low, and even worse, it is falling. But that does not mean that markets do not exist for quality goods. As long as there are substantial numbers of affluent consumers—and there are in Peru—significant markets exist for quality imports.

Averages are like the man with one foot in a tub of scalding water and the other foot in a tub of ice water. On the average, he is comfortable! The same principle applies to marketing. Average incomes might convince marketers not to consider exporting to a country, but using market data in that manner can be misleading. The relevant questions are: Do substantial numbers of consumers exist with sufficient income to buy the product? Do adequate distribution channels exist to handle and sell the products properly? For food products in Peru, the answer to both questions is yes. Or perhaps I should say the answer is *si*.

Another discovery in Peru was Inca-Cola. In distribution and taste, it is similar to Pepsi-Cola or Coca-Cola. There is a major difference, however. Inca-Cola is a beautiful, clear gold color. You'll find it on every street corner with vendors who walk around selling the product and, in many places, in coolers that reminded me of the Coca-Cola distribution system when I was a child. I'm always amazed at how the distribution systems of developing countries parallel the marketing and distribution common in the United States when I first began learning about marketing a few decades ago.

Inca-Cola is sold in cans and bottles and at soda fountains similar to how Coca-Cola and Pepsi-Cola are sold. I am told that Inca-Cola sells more than Pepsi and rivals Coke closely. Inca-Cola is such a success story that it is now exported to other countries, including the United States, mostly in southern states with large numbers of Latinos.

There are always lessons that can be learned when we discover successes such as Inca-Cola. One is that the little firms of the world can take on the giants and do well. It is interesting that the translucent or clear attribute of Inca-Cola has a parallel in the clear colas introduced in the United States recently. The other lesson to be learned from Inca-Cola is the importance of understanding the culture of a society and relating products to it. The Inca Indians were renowned for their use of gold artifacts. Tying the golden color of a soft drink to the ancient values related to Inca gold is good marketing (and good soda, as well)!

## Human ATMs at Every Corner

One of the most interesting sights in Peru (and in numerous other countries) is a person with a large roll of bills at every street corner.

172

As you stop at the light, these individuals offer to change currency for you. They are trading hard currencies of the world into local currencies.

In the United States, we have an automatic teller machine (ATM) on almost every corner, it seems. In Peru, it is a human performing some of the same functions. Why?

Inflation is the answer. When inflation is several thousand percent a year, getting paid in local currency and holding it overnight means you lose a lot of pay. So you change it into a hard currency—probably U.S. dollars—which you keep until the moment you want to buy something. That is why you need a money changer at every corner, and you'll find plenty of these human ATMs in Peru. How it all works is incredibly complex, but it works.

There is a lesson to be learned here, too. I have talked to some businesspeople who have written off doing business in Latin America. Inflation is too difficult to deal with, they often say. Yet if you go to Peru, you will see B. F. Goodrich selling tires, Johnson and Johnson selling baby products, and many other global firms operating profitably. Problems such as rapid inflation have solutions. Successful people simply have to learn those solutions.

## *Mugged in the Marketplace*

I stayed in a fine hotel in Lima. When I mentioned to my hosts that I probably would go jogging in the nearby area, my hosts immediately forbade me to do that. Too dangerous, they said, and offered to take me to a suburban area and drive alongside me if I insisted on jogging. This made an impression on me, but I still wanted to see all parts of the city.

My hosts, including one of the top marketing professors in Peru, spent a great amount of time taking me to various parts of the city and meeting business and educational personalities, as well as touring the good and the bad of the city—and experiencing some of Peru's outstanding restaurants!

# PERU
*A Study in Contrasts*

One of the places I especially wanted to see was the central market. Especially on Saturdays, it is a throbbing area of the city with thousands of people buying and selling food, clothing, household goods, and most anything else you might imagine. It was one of my highest priorities to see as a marketing professor.

"Not safe for a gringo," my hosts suggested, but I insisted and they agreed to go with me. They warned me to take no wallet, no ring, no watch, no credit cards, and no money—and to dress simply. I followed the instructions with one exception. I wore an inexpensive Casio watch.

No sooner was I out of the car and into the marketplace when I was hit with incredible speed by a group of young men. They said nothing, just quickly grabbed me and tore the watch from my arm. I was lucky that I had such a cheap watch. If the band had not broken easily, they would have used their knives quickly to cut the watch—and part of my arm.

Although I regretted losing the watch, I was lucky not to be hurt. And I have to say that I had a certain admiration for the young thieves' execution of their strategy. They watched for the perfect time, when I was surrounded by other people. It was so quick I could never have identified any of them. Later, when I had nothing more to steal, I watched the eyes of similar groups of thieves who carefully studied the gringo who walked through the crowd to see if there was anything else to steal. I learned a lot that day. You can tell a lot about a person's intentions by studying closely his or her eyes.

My professor friend wanted to buy me a watch to replace my stolen one. We stopped at one of the shops in the marketplace selling Casio watches for only five dollars. I did not find the exact style I had lost and explained what had happened to the proprietor of the shop. He listened carefully to my description of the watch I wanted and replied, "Give me about five minutes. I think I can have a watch just like the one you lost!"

## *Communism and Terrorism*

In the first chapter of this book, I listed the fall of communism as one of the most influential events of this century. The effects are not felt just in Communist countries; they are felt in many developing countries. This was tragically obvious to me in Peru.

Peru, like many countries in South America, Asia, and Africa, had strong support from the Soviets and other Communist countries. The support was intended to overthrow their governments. Often the support was financial and provided the livelihood of terrorists.

Now that financial and philosophical support has vanished for the terrorist groups, they have had to find a new way to support themselves. Sometimes they still claim to be terrorists for philosophical reasons, but as a practical matter they are simply thieves. But they are somewhat organized, well-armed, and very dangerous thieves.

The terrorists have taken over some universities in Peru, demanding that students and professors do whatever they say. In other places they control highways in areas called "Sherwood Forests." The thieves use rocks to block highways and when motorists stop to move them, the thieves mob the motorists, stealing anything of value and often killing the motorists.

Not all of the violence in Peru is by terrorists. Often it is committed by people who are simply poor or greedy. The violence and crime are huge problems for businesses who must hire bodyguards and drive bulletproof cars. It is a problem for ordinary citizens who must live in fear and accept great restrictions on their mobility. Partly, the violence can be blamed on poverty. Sadly, it is also simply a part of the culture.

I could not help but wonder if the same type of culture is not becoming widespread in the United States. Poverty is a cause of violence, of course, but I fear that shooting people and other forms of violence are becoming accepted, almost condoned, activities by some leaders. An injustice is sometimes offered as an acceptable reason for retaliation with violence or disregard for the law. When I was in Colorado recently, I watched the trial of two teenagers. When a state trooper had attempted to arrest them for a traffic violation, one of the teenagers pulled a gun and killed the officer. In many areas of our cities (and rural areas), violence and high-fire-power weapons are accepted as just part of life (or death).

I saw that phenomenon rampant in Peru (and it exists in other countries, of course). I fear that the United States is developing the same approach to violence and terrorism, at least by many young people and some older people who accept and reinforce such behavior.

If you want to know what life could be like in the United States, visit Peru. It is a great country in many ways. It is possible to have a good quality of life, but how good can the quality of life be when you run the risk of carjackings, murders, and terrorism by organized and well-armed gangs at almost every intersection?

Every country offers a lot of lessons to be learned. Countries such as Peru provide a great many contrasts and show us things to emulate and things to avoid. That's the way I see it . . . from the edge.

# 14

# CANADA

*Vacation to Learn about*
*Cross-Cultural Understanding*

**If you have not yet planned your next summer vacation,** you may want to cross the edge of the world and visit another country. If you have children, it could be an opportunity to help them understand some fundamentals of global business.

China, Japan, or Germany might be the most educational places to visit. If your checkbook or Gold Card argue against that plan, there is a foreign country only a few hours' drive from much of the United States. Canada—the nearest "edge of the world"—is a good place to take your family for a vacation with a purpose: cross-cultural understanding.

### Learn to Earn

When you take your family to any foreign country, it is a good time to teach basic economic principles such as foreign exchange. Learn to earn and you may improve your lifestyle. Teach your children to learn to earn and you may improve your future.

Traveling to a foreign country—even though Canada may not seem so foreign—is a good time to develop an improved understanding of what is required to be successful in the new global economy. Make sure your family (and you!) understands why the Canadian dollar buys less than the U.S. dollar. Check the rate throughout your trip to observe daily fluctuations and how they relate to world events and economic policies. It may be easier to understand rate fluctuations in Canadian dollars and U.S. dollars than fluctuations with the yen or the mark, and the principles that are learned are the same. One way to increase your earnings in a global economy is to understand the value of a country's currency in relation to others. Some people make a lot of money directly by engaging in currency trading, but everybody indirectly can improve their economic position by knowing the factors that cause value to be associated with money.

## NAFTA and Intermarket Segmentation

Ask people in Canada what they think of the North American Free Trade Agreement. It could be an important influence on your own prosperity regardless of where you live. You may find less support for NAFTA in Canada than in the U.S. If all goes according to plan, however, most trade barriers between Canada and the United States are scheduled to end by 1999. Canada and the United States are already the largest trading partnership in the world; NAFTA should only strengthen this alliance.

Market segmentation differs when applied in a country with approximately 10 percent of the population of the United States. A smaller population base has made it more difficult for Canadian firms to use market segmentation as effectively as U.S. firms.

One of the advantages of NAFTA is the ability to appeal to similar segments of the population regardless of where those cus-

tomers may be located. The concept of intermarket segmentation, which we described in chapter 12, is very appropriate when analyzing North American markets. It is possible, indeed probable, that customer segments in Montana and Alberta or Ontario and Michigan will be much more efficiently addressed in marketing programs than placing customers together in Alberta and Ontario as a customer segment.

## *Parlez-vous Français?*

You can already see the effects of NAFTA in many American grocery stores. Recently, I saw Dare cookies in a local grocery store with ingredients labeled in both French and English. What's happening here? An appeal to the American city's huge French population? No, the cookies are imported from Canada where bilingual packaging is mandatory.

Firms based in the United States that want to export to Canada will also need to learn how to do bilingual packaging, use visual language, and employ other methods of cross-border marketing. Borden and Wyandot Foods are major U.S. snack producers. They are different types of firms in that Borden is part of a huge publicly held corporation and Wyandot is a highly focused, privately held corporation. Both, however, might benefit from more cross-border sales.

One of the objectives I hope to accomplish with this book is to overcome ethnocentricity. I hope to challenge the complacency about global trade opportunities that we often see among managers and workers. When asked about specific labeling, packaging, or product modifications that might be needed to attract foreign markets, I have seen many people shrug their heads and say, "It is too much trouble."

I hope you can tell as you come near the end of this book that I feel passionately about the need for viewing the world and not just our own nation as our marketplace. Every business owner, every manager, every worker, and indeed every citizen needs to understand and be responsive to the needs of markets in many countries.

For those who do not make such efforts, I fear that their economic future is bleak. Part of the reason for this book is so that people will know how to make their own economic future more secure, rather than bleak.

Many workers and managers who fail to learn languages or at least make effective use of those who do know them increasingly will have difficulty finding employers for their labors. Some individuals will lose their jobs because they or their employers do not understand how to be effective in global markets. Such individuals may well ask government or business to help them find a job or provide welfare payments. For individuals who have not made the effort to be globally skilled, the answer given to them may simply be, "It is too much trouble."

## *Cross-Cultural Analysis*

You may want to use your trip to Canada to do some cross-cultural analysis. The concept is from the discipline of anthropology and one that is very useful in marketing. If you have survived reading this book and want to study the concept of cross-cultural analysis in more depth, I would suggest the chapter on culture in *Consumer Behavior* (with James Engel and Paul Miniard). In plain language, cross-cultural analysis means trying to understand the similarities and differences among people of different cultures. The similarities are so great between people in Canada and the United States that the differences are sometimes ignored.

Canadians are more law abiding and more accepting of the federal government's role, a cultural norm traced back to differences in the two countries' histories. The Royal Canadian Mounted Police brought law and order to the Canadian frontier with a reputation that the Mounties always find the criminal. In the American frontier, the only law was the law of the six guns of cowboys and independent marshals. If you violate the speed limit while visiting Canada, the Mounties will still find you!

You can see differences in the attitude toward government in many areas. In Canada, the courts are perceived as an arm of the state, while in the United States, courts are perceived as a check on the powers of the state. Lobbyists are found less in Canada because politicians toe the party line. We have more than seven thousand lobbying organizations registered in the U.S. Congress since legislators can vote more independently and are therefore more influenced by lobbying.

The biggest difference between Canada and the United States may be in the health system. Both are similar in that they have good doctors, good hospitals, and good access to quality health care if you should need emergency care. But the similarities end when it comes to financing and universal access for the nation's citizens. When you visit Canada, do not miss the chance to ask the people you meet about their views of the Canadian health system. This could be valuable input to your own thinking about the changes initiated by President and Mrs. Clinton in the U.S. health system.


## *President's Choice*

Perhaps no one enjoys visiting retailers and other businesses as much as I do when visiting another country and even in my own country. I love to spend time in stores, watching and talking with customers. That is the only way to truly understand consumer behavior. One of the trends I have observed in Canadian supermarkets is the tendency of consumers to choose the President's Choice. It is a trend that started in Canada but is so important that it is the focus of articles in the *Wall Street Journal.* It is a reason that stock prices dropped substantially in recent years for RJ Reynolds and other firms that depend on the marketing of major consumer brands.

When you visit Canada, try to visit Loblaws or one of the other major supermarkets. Loblaws developed the President's Choice brand for use in its stores and is now remarketing it to some other stores. President's Choice is a premium store brand offered at a popular price. It is different from previous store brands. President's Choice leads the trend that is beginning to occur in other areas of North America. Consumers are buying more store brands that are often better products than manufacturers' brands, in better designed packages, and with as good or better advertising.

Canada is more advanced in the use of store brands. At Loblaws you will see how a retailer can change the balance of power (and perhaps benefit consumers) with a store brand such as President's Choice. Compared to manufacturer brands, store brands in the United States were usually of minimal or mixed product quality, with inferior package design, and little or no advertising support.

The Canadians changed those principles, and the changes have not been lost on all American firms. We have recently seen

Kroger brands growing in popularity because of a major redesign and repositioning program. Numerous regional grocery chains are experiencing a colossal success with the World Classics store brand, distributed by Topko Associates in Skokie, Illinois. Not only is the packaging attractive, but the products are wonderful. My question is, Should the stores be selling their private labels for more or less than the price of the national brands?

Those successes could have been predicted by anyone who understands cross-cultural analysis by visiting Canada, where good store brands typically outsell manufacturer brands; and they don't always sell for less than national brands. At Loblaws, try the President's Choice brand of cookies. Canadians told me they were better than Nabisco. I tried them, and I agree! Back in the United States, my wife and I buy World Classics chocolate chip cookies, not because they are cheaper, but because we believe they taste better than some of the better known national brands. It is a new world of marketing when we consumers think of store brands as superior to manufacturer brands—and one in which the people caught sleeping during the change were those who had not been to Canada and watched the trend occurring there first.

If you are a globally oriented person, you probably already realize that no country has a monopoly on innovation. Part of the ethnocentricity trap for American management is the belief in the NIH syndrome. NIH stands for "Not Invented Here." The NIH syndrome causes many ethnocentric American managers to delay progress or fail to reap the benefits of innovation. Too often I have seen advertising executives look at ads from Canada, Australia, the United Kingdom, South Africa, or other places where English is spoken. Frequently they will be captivated by such ads but then quickly add, "They would not work in the U.S. We must make our own ads." Such executives are often wrong. Managers in many other countries of the world have demonstrated their ability to borrow, adapt, and translate the best and first ideas from wherever they find them. American managers who are prepared for leadership in the twenty-first century must be able to do the same. An example can be found in the Work Mate, a product invented originally by Black and Decker's Canadian subsidiary. It became a great success in the United States, although the U.S. parent waited years before introducing the Canadian product to U.S. markets.

### All Work and No Play Makes Jack a Dull Boy!

In my enthusiasm to encourage you to visit Canada for educational reasons, you might conclude that the trip would be all business and no fun. Not true, of course. Some of the most spectacular scenery in the world can be found in the Canadian Rockies, especially at Lake Louise. Nearby, the Old West still lives, especially during the Calgary Stampede. Vancouver has the best of everything—mountains, ocean, flowers, and the excitement of an ethnically diverse, cosmopolitan city.

Wherever you go in Canada, be sure to visit one of twenty-four Harry Rosen stores—possibly the best men's clothing retailer in the world. We were so excited about the level of service as well as the quality of the clothing that we made Harry Rosen the subject of one of the cases in the textbook my wife and I wrote, *Contemporary Cases in Consumer Behavior.* Harry Rosen has become a good friend and has taught me much about men's fashion. He appears in a series of Harry Rosen ads and has become one of the most recognized men in Canada—and one of the best dressed. While you won't find him tailoring too many suits anymore, you will see him wandering through his stores, making sure customers and staff are happy. The men's divisions at the Limited might take lessons from Harry Rosen—both the store and the man.

My favorite area of Canada is the rugged but economically depressed coastal region of the Maritimes. If you visit Nova Scotia, bring back some kelp—the tasty (but salty) seaweed that proves we can live healthfully from the ocean if we run out of water to irrigate our agricultural land. Perhaps this is a new product introduction for Worthington Foods, America's largest marketer of vegetarian foods.

# CANADA
*Vacation to Learn about Cross-Cultural Understanding*


To really feel as if you are in foreign country, visit Montreal and Quebec. Don't worry if you don't speak French. Most people also speak English and will do so if they realize you are from the United States rather than Canada. A visit to Quebec allows you to experience the French culture without having to cross the Atlantic.

Americans who believe in cultural diversity will love Toronto, a fantastically Euro-Asian-American city. When you are in downtown Toronto, be sure to visit Eaton Centre—an excellent example of revitalization of major city central business districts through the use of malls. In many ways, it was the prototype for Columbus, Ohio's, City Center. Together they are two of the most successful downtown developments in North America.

If you are a fan of good food, you'll love Toronto. Toronto has great restaurants (but not as great as Montreal!), good theater and comedy clubs, and of course the CN Tower—a romantic place for a 360-degree tour of the city without leaving your table.

We live in a global marketplace. One way to develop a global perspective on a budget is to visit Canada with a purpose—the purpose to better understand cross-cultural consumer values, political/legal environments, currency and exchange rates, bilingual marketing, ethnic diversity, and other topics that help you prosper in the new global environment.

That's the way I see it . . . from the nearest edge of the world!

185

# 15

# MEXICO

*Next NAFTA Neighbor?*

**Cancun. Acapulco. Puerto Vallarta. Tijuana.** Most Americans know something about at least one country in the world. And almost everyone has heard of the resort cities in Mexico. Many have visited some or all of them. Many might say there is little need to write about Mexico because most people in the United States already know a lot about their neighbors south of the border.

But do they? Do we really understand the relative potential for growth in Mexico compared to the United States? Do we really understand the similarities between the United States and Mexico as well as the differences? Do we really understand the impact on business realities created by the developing nature of Mexican-U.S. partnerships of many kinds? Do we really understand the growing nucleus of cultural-economic ties between the two nations along with Canada that are likely to provide leadership for the Americas in the twenty-first century?

Tourism is important when thinking about Mexico, but it is an industry about which many Americans already have some understanding. It bothers me when I see young men diving off high cliffs into the ocean in order to entertain and earn money from tourists. I am told that young men would be doing the same thing even if there were no tourists, but it still bothers me to believe that *yanqui* money may be encouraging a dangerous activity that might result in permanent paralysis or even death.

Many tourists are also bothered by the contrasts found in Mexico. It is not unusual to stay in a beautiful, luxurious hotel. Across the street or around the corner are likely to be families living in abject poverty, perhaps in a squatters' area called *colonia,* subsisting with little food and few clothes in houses made of cardboard and without sanitation facilities. One has to question whether tourism has made much of a contribution to the quality of life for most residents of Mexico's tourism cities, let alone the 20 million or more people packed into hot and heavily polluted Mexico City.

To me, the much more important issues to be considered when thinking of Mexico are not about the events experienced by most tourists, even though tourism is an important source of currency. The more important issues to analyze involve the growing importance of Mexico as part of the North American market for both production and consumption of a wide range of goods and services.

## NAFTA: To Be or Not To Be?

As this book was being written, President Bill Clinton was requesting ratification of the North American Free Trade Agreement, a treaty that would lower or eliminate most of the trade barriers between Mexico, Canada, and the United States. The U.S. Congress was beginning to consider the many issues involved in ratification. As you read this chapter, you will know whether the treaty was passed, rejected, or delayed. My bet is the last of those options is the most likely for quite a while before eventual passage.

# MEXICO
## Next NAFTA Neighbor?


In one sense, it does not matter whether or not NAFTA is passed. Many of the changes in both countries and the increases in economic cooperation are inevitable. They were occurring at a rapid rate before NAFTA and will continue whether or not NAFTA is ratified.

Most of the opposition to NAFTA arises from fear of losing jobs to Mexico. Labor unions are opposed to the treaty, fearing permanent layoffs from jobs that might be lost to Mexico, resulting in a decline in membership. They are right, of course. Some jobs will be lost to Mexico. The type of jobs most likely to be lost are those in labor-intensive, repetitive manufacturing operations. That is to be expected. Economist Joseph Schumpeter called it creative destruction and said progress is achieved through the elimination of mostly low-skill jobs and creation of mostly valuable jobs.

I find several faults with the "lost jobs" argument. The first fault is that those jobs would have been lost, regardless of whether or not NAFTA was passed. High labor–content manufacturing jobs are in the process of moving rapidly from high-wage countries to low-wage countries on a global basis. That has to scare labor unions.

The reality is not whether manufacturing jobs will stay in the United States or be transferred to Mexico. The reality is whether such jobs will transfer to Mexico or to some other country. The only other alternative for such jobs is for Americans to be willing to accept a wage of a few dollars a day, an alternative I doubt most Americans will find acceptable.

The second fault with the "lost jobs" argument against NAFTA is that when jobs are lost to Mexico, they are also created in the United States. The number of jobs created is probably larger than the number lost. No one knows the exact ratio, but studies that appear credible estimate the ratio at about three jobs gained for each one lost. How likely do you think that is?

Furthermore, the jobs lost are likely to be the high labor--content, repetitive manufacturing and assembly jobs. The jobs gained are likely to be in firms that are successful in manufacturing in Mexico but planning, managing, selling, and distributing in the United States and other parts of the global marketplace. Thus, the jobs gained are likely to be in accounting, management, sales, research and development, logistics, and similar skills; i.e., high-paying jobs in which to place university graduates.

The third and greatest fault with the "lost jobs" argument is that it ignores the "found sales" effects of NAFTA. Do we want the jobs that are inevitably going to be lost from the United States to go to Asia or Africa or to Mexico and other Latin American countries? It is the Latin neighbors that are more likely to be sources of demand for goods and services made in the United States.

One of the best observers of this process is Sidney Weintraub, a professor and Latin American scholar at the University of Texas. He sums up the process succinctly: "When Latins sell to us, they buy even more back. When Asians sell to us, they buy from Japan. And when Europeans sell to us, they buy from each other. Latin America is our best opportunity."

## *Mexican Markets*

Mexico is a country 20 percent the physical size of the United States but with a population more than 35 percent of the United States (90 million people in Mexico compared to 252 million in the United States). Life expectancy is a little lower in Mexico (68 for males, 76 for females) than in the United States (72 for males, 79 for females); but the birth rates are much higher in Mexico (29 per 1,000 population in 1991) than in the United States (15 per 1,000 in 1991). As a consequence, the population of Mexico is growing at the rate of 2.2 percent per year as compared to .8 percent annually in the United States in the first part of the 1990s. That number is expected to drop to .6 percent annually by the end of the 1990s.

You can see why firms that want to sell cars, building materials, furniture, telephones, banking services, and a wide array of other goods and services have their eyes on Mexico. As a point of comparison, Canada is larger in size than the United States but has only a little more than 10 percent of the population (26.8 million people). People live longer in Canada (74 years for males, 81 for females) than in the United States or Mexico, have about the same birth rate as the United States, and a slightly higher growth in population (1.1 percent annually). Mexican workers have a lower literacy rate (87 percent) than American workers (97 percent), but Canadians have a higher literacy rate (99 percent) than either country. Mexicans work longer (47.1 hours per week) than do Americans (41 hours per week), while Canadians have it a bit easier (38.6 hours per week) than either country.

The United States sells more than $15 billion of machinery to Mexico, more than $4 billion of transport equipment, $4.4 billion of manufacturing goods, and billions more of chemicals, food, materials, and other products. Firms and individuals from the United States have invested (as of 1991) nearly ten times as much capital in the manufacturing, petroleum, and finance industries of Canada as they have in Mexico. But I expect the higher growth rate in the population of Mexico to attract relatively more capital to Mexico in the future, especially with the Mexican government's recent relaxation of controls on foreign investment.

The bottom line is that U.S. firms focusing on their own bottom lines will increasingly be focusing on Mexican markets. In Mexico City, the U.S. Department of Agriculture recently sponsored the Festival Alimentos y Bebidas. Mexico is already one of the United States's largest export markets for products such as red meat, processed and dairy food products, poultry, and snack foods. But many more U.S. firms were there studying the opportunities. The food products exhibited were as diverse as fast food from White Castle, America's original hamburger chain, to Worthington Foods, America's leading marketer of meat analogs and other vegetarian foods.

## *Manufacturing in Mexico*

Many manufacturers may be attracted to Mexico because of the lure of cheap labor. Already established, reputable U.S. firms stay because of the availability of quality labor. When I was in Tokyo, Hong Kong, and Singapore preparing to write this book, I was told in each city that the biggest worry of industrial firms in the Orient is that their jobs will soon be replaced by Mexican workers if NAFTA is ratified.

The greatest concentration of U.S.-based manufacturing is along the border in factories, or *maquiladoras*, which assemble products for export outside Mexico. Those factories were the primary foreign investments permitted by the Mexican government until more favorable policies were adopted in 1989 and the movement toward NAFTA began. However, the policies continue to be controversial, and for good reason. Labor problems have often been stormy, with labor turnover rates of 10–12 percent per month. Many of the problems are attributed to the fact that *maquiladora* plants are generally operated by the domestic division of U.S. firms rather than the international division. I believe that domestic managers of U.S. firms are often less sensitive to cultural differences than are managers in the international division.

The lack of good relationships between management and labor as well as the constant need to train new workers make the cost of hiring labor much higher than the apparent wage rate. Professor George Baker at the University of California estimates that a firm with those kinds of problems may have actual labor costs of $10 an hour even if it pays an apparent wage rate of only $1.50 per hour.

Firms that understand how to manage "over the edge" pay special attention to the culture of their workers. Effective managers in Mexico and other Latin American countries I have visited often view themselves as father figures rather than bosses. They emphasize the role of instructor or teacher for the workers. Ken Franklin, who manages assembly plants in Juárez's giant Bermudez Industrial

191

Park, visits the production line every day at 6 a.m. to greet each worker individually. "In Mexico, *everything* is a personal matter," he says. "But a lot of managers don't get it."

## The Jolly Green Giant

Green Giant is a U.S. firm that attracted a lot of attention when it moved some of its food processing operations from California to Mexico, near Irapuato. It says that the move was made because of closer proximity to eastern U.S. markets and the year-round growing season. Wages vary depending on the type of work done, but Pillsbury, which owns Green Giant, reports that wage rates average eighty-three cents an hour, excluding benefits.

Some of the *maquiladora* workers are doing jobs once done by Green Giant's plant in Watsonville, California. The Teamsters Union, which represented the workers in California, claims that Green Giant saved $6 million a year by moving to Irapuato. The company claims that it pays bonuses, health benefits, and other costly items that understate the wage rates. I have not verified the claims of the opposing views, but I happened to be visiting in California at the time the Watsonville plant was closed.

I listened to local news coverage as TV news reporters interviewed the laid off workers, most of whom had immigrated to the United States from Mexico. A plant had been built in the United States by Green Giant that paid wages so high that workers were attracted to emigrate from Mexico. Because of its high wages (perhaps encouraged by unions, which later objected to the closing), the plant was no longer competitive and had to be closed. The company built the plant in Mexico to employ the same type of workers that had originally immigrated to the United States.

It is a strange cycle of events, isn't it? It illustrates the nature of global economic relationships as well as, if not better than, any example I can describe. It also raises an interesting question about the

192

potential effects of free trade. If both Mexico and the United States had never erected the trade and investment barriers, would it not have been more efficient for Green Giant to build its plant in Mexico the first time?

## *Detroit South*

Mexico is emerging as the home of a low-cost, high-quality work force. Ironically, location adjacent to that type of labor force may be a major reason U.S. auto manufacturers may be better able to survive than German or Japanese firms, which must rely on labor pools that are either high cost in some countries or low quality in others.

"Detroit South" was the title given to Mexico in a *Business Week* cover story that documented well the advantages of Mexican auto manufacturing. A quality edge for Mexican workers is obtained with Japanese-style manufacturing methods. The quality teams feature highly trained workers in small teams who can interchange duties and monitor each other's quality. They even sing songs—Japanese style—such as "Planta Mía" extolling the virtues of their company in Spanish. With this quality work force and quality work processes, it is not surprising that General Motor's Ramos Arizpe plant has become the number one plant in company-wide quality records.

What do you get when you hire Mexican workers? The answer is people who are highly motivated and generally younger and more flexible than U.S. auto workers who (I'm told) can learn new model changeovers and procedures three times faster than Detroit workers. They are nonunion and are willing to work hard for one dollar per hour. You can see why GM, Ford, Chrysler, and others have gone far beyond the *maquiladoras* to make major investments in plants and people in Mexico.

If there is one lesson to be learned from visiting Mexico, it is that the importance of autos is increasing in Mexico's economy and declining in the United States. In the past, the auto industry was reported to provide one out of eight jobs in the American economy, either directly or indirectly. That ratio is declining fast, and I see few economists or business leaders addressing it realistically. Did paying twenty-four dollars an hour in the auto industry and maintaining highly restrictive work rules eventually eliminate those jobs? Could it have been avoided by a better understanding of the realities of global competition and production?

Those are part of the trends that are leading to what I call an Age of Nonemployment. The United States and other industrialized economies no longer need a high proportion of human beings in order to produce or buy the nation's goods and services. Nonemployment does not arise from lack of economic growth or failure of a particular political party to fine-tune monetary policies.

The Age of Nonemployment has been created by structural changes in the nature of production of goods and services that are more affected by global economic principles than economics of business cycles that have been taught in economic departments and business schools for so many decades. Some alternative arrangements are needed to solve the problems created by the Age of Nonemployment. I believe there are answers to the dilemma—perhaps that will be my next book!

One more key fact attracts auto manufacturers to Mexico. What is one of the major ways Mexicans will spend the money from their new jobs? You guessed it. Cars! And trucks! *Business Week* published estimates that car and light truck sales growth in the U.S. would increase only .7 percent (and actually decrease in Canada) between the years 1985 and 2000. In Mexico, however, the growth rate is expected to change 435.7 percent during the same time period.

Why are American firms moving so rapidly to Mexico to manufacture their products? Partly for quality and cost reasons. With an eye to the future, however, the reason is more often because Mexico is the market of the future for North American firms.

# MEXICO
## *Next NAFTA Neighbor?*

Cantina del Rio: Mexico or Columbus?

## *North of the Border*

One of the reasons for visiting any country is to bring back things—whether those things are food, souvenirs, or ideas. For many Americans, *piñatas*, *fajitas*, and *margaritas* are just a few of the trademarks of Mexican culture that have been transported north of the border.

One of those who discovered Mexican culture was Dan Evans, chief executive officer of the Bob Evans restaurant and food company. Famed for its sausage, the firm acquired a similar firm in Texas, which placed Dan Evans and other company officials both south and north of the border long enough to acquire a taste for Mexican cuisine. In the Midwest, there were not many places to satisfy that hunger other than Taco Bell. Dan found a top operator of Mexican restaurants to act as consultant and provide recipes. Together they set out on an expedition throughout Mexico. Driving a sixteen-wheeler, they stopped every place they found artifacts they thought would enhance the image of an authentic Mexican restaurant and transplanted them to states far north of the border.

Faded neon signs from *cantinas, cerveza* signs from along the road, and colorful mosaics by Mexican artists were just a few of the items they loaded into the truck before heading home. I am told that they wanted to buy a door from one house, offering the owner one hundred dollars in cash. He immediately offered to sell them the windows too; they probably could have gotten the rest of the house if they had tried!

The result: Cantina Del Rio, a successful chain of Mexican restaurants that proves that *norteamericanos* can absorb a lot from a new culture. The recipes may be a little milder than they would be south of the border, but the buildings are so authentic that they caused more than one city's zoning council to ask that the rambling, faded, and sometimes dilapidated exterior appearance be a little milder also.

I first visited Mexico more than two decades ago. One of the things I observed as part of the culture was the *siesta*, that sleepy time after lunch when people let the meal properly digest. I have always felt that a siesta was one of life's most pleasant luxuries, even though I only rarely found time to experience it properly. I objected strenuously when students in my afternoon marketing class experimented with the phenomenon, occasionally stopping class to remind them that siestas were not permitted in the United States.

When I go to Mexico today, I do not find many people taking siestas anymore. The sleepy lifestyle of the siesta has given way to the exuberant, hard-working economy of a country rapidly moving toward the twenty-first century.

## *Thief with a Conscience*

My wife and I landed at the favorite Mexican city of many Americans—Acapulco—and quickly found a taxi to take us to the airport.

# MEXICO
## Next NAFTA Neighbor?

I threw our travel bag into the back seat so I could take out the hotel reservations. I rarely know the name of the hotel to tell the
driver until I check the reservations. This happens because I have
the world's most reliable travel agent. Jerry Dye of University
Travel has booked travel arrangements for me for more than
twenty-five years, and as incredible as this statement may seem, he
has never made a mistake. So I pulled the name of the hotel from
the bag, gave it to the driver, and we were on our way to the hotel. I
paid the driver. He gave me a receipt and we were ready for the fun
and sun of Acapulco. We thoroughly enjoyed ourselves for three
days until we decided to do some sightseeing. When I tried to take
the camera from the travel bag, I quickly realized that I had no bag.

You guessed the problem. I had left the bag in the back of the
taxi. Not only did the bag contain the camera, but it had an envelope of Mexican currency I had left over from a previous trip. Not a
large amount but enough for me to assume that I would not get
the bag back. The bag also included some important papers I
needed for the rest of the trip as well as sunglasses, cosmetics, and
other items.

I asked the concierge for help, and she asked me the name of
the taxi company. Would you remember the name of the company
or the driver if you landed in Acapulco for a few days of relaxation?
(Oops! I mean, research.) Then my wife reminded me that I put the
receipt in a jacket that I had not worn since landing in Mexico. I
found the receipt, tracked down the taxi company, and was informed they had many bags in their lost and found department.
The papers were my major concern. I did not really expect to re-
cover the cash or the camera.

We found the bag. The papers were there and I breathed a
sigh of relief. The envelope of cash was there with not a peso miss-
ing. So were the sunglasses and other items. Even more amazing,
there was the camera case, which I unzipped to check the camera. I
did a double take. In place of my Minolta was an ancient Kodak
Instamatic.

The driver said he had no knowledge about the camera switch, and to this day I have no way of knowing how the switch occurred. The Minolta was not an expensive camera, even though it was much better than the Instamatic. It does not seem likely that someone who would switch the cameras just to steal the better camera would leave the cash and other more valuable contents. Did the taxi driver need a new camera? Did another passenger go through the bag and switch the cameras before the bag was turned over to the driver? Did the lost and found department take an old abandoned Kodak and make the switch? I'll never know. I only know that apparently the person who stole my camera took pity on an American tourist who would have been stranded in Mexico on a vacation with no camera. I guess I was fortunate to encounter a thief with a conscience!

My only clue to the identity of the thief is the undeveloped roll of film—which I developed—that was in the camera. I do have some nice prints of the Pacific Coast apparently taken by a Mexican family on vacation near Acapulco!

I was pleased to get the travel bag back. I could not help but wonder if the same outcome would have occurred in Chicago or New York. If you left a bag containing cash and a camera in the back seat of a taxi in an American city, how likely would you be to get the bag returned complete with cash and an old Instamatic a few days later?

There is a lesson to be learned in all of this. Always keep the receipt from your taxi when you land at an airport. It also might not be a bad idea always to check the back seat before departing the taxi!

That's the way I see things . . . from the "near edge" of the world in Mexico.

# 16

# OVER THE EDGE

**"You've Come a Long Way, Baby,"** says one cigarette marketer in its advertising. The same could be said about travel since the early days when explorers were afraid of sailing over the edge. They heeded the warning, "Beware, for beyond the edge, there be dragons."

In their thinking about countries beyond the borders of the United States, an increasing number of people are willing to go over the edge, to see what is on the other side. In an increasing number of companies, managers and other employees are beginning to develop a global perspective. I hope the previous fifteen chapters of this book have helped you develop a global perspective.

Providing global perspectives about business is the purpose of this book. Having a global perspective is no guarantee of success for you individually or for your company. But it is an indispensable edge in gaining survival and prosperity in today's globalized economy.

The lessons learned from traveling with me vicariously to each of the countries have, perhaps, stimulated your thinking. I hope you formed conclusions not only about each of the countries but about how lessons learned in those countries can be applied domestically. Learning about the best and worst to be found in each country can lead to global perspectives on many areas of marketing and business strategy. Learning those perspectives may give you an extra edge over others who lack such global perspectives, whether your interest be personal or professional. The concepts in this book are presented as perspectives to enhance the effectiveness of the basic functions in business; they can provide a special insight to help you compete in a changing global economy.

## *Give Us Our Daily Coke*

There is an old story about an executive at Coca-Cola who was concerned about the slowing growth of the product worldwide. During a staff meeting to discuss solutions to the problem, a bright young assistant offered the following suggestion: The company should approach the pope and ask him to change the most frequently offered prayer of the Church from "Give us our daily bread" to "Give us our daily Coca-Cola."

The executive approached the pope, according to the story, and made the request. When His Holiness informed the executive of the enormous costs of changing prayer books, the executive suggested that the company would provide a grant of $1 million to defray costs. His Holiness replied that the executive should return the next day to learn of his decision. When the executive returned, the pope informed him that the Church could not consider such a request.

The executive upped the price dramatically, first offering $10 million and finally offering $50 million if the prayer used throughout the world could simply be changed to "Give us our daily Coca-Cola." His Holiness finally told the executive he would pray about the decision and contact him later. As soon as the executive left the Vatican, the pope called the financial secretary and asked, "How many years do we have to run on the Wonder Bread contract?"

While the story is told in jest, if there were anyone who would ever try the strategy, it might be Sergio Zyman, the chief marketing officer of Coca-Cola. I think Coca-Cola is a contender for the most global of America's major corporations, with 80 percent of its earnings and 90 percent of its earnings growth from overseas markets. In spite of that impressive record, when Mr. Zyman assumed the chief marketing slot at Coca-Cola, he lost no time intensifying the focus on global markets. Four days after assuming the number one marketing position at Coke, Mr. Zyman set in motion a bold and sweeping reorganization of Coke to make it even more globally oriented. In a 1993 *Advertising Age* article describing the changes, one analyst commented, "If you have to pick a place, the action's overseas for Coca-Cola."

I find more and more firms heading in the direction of Coca-Cola—change to be globally oriented or assume the risk of becoming the dinosaur. That seems to be the best advice that I could give most firms and their employees. Increasingly, the ability to think globally is one of the ways a firm can increase its profits in the face of slow-growth domestic markets. And the people who will receive the most personal rewards are increasingly those who can think globally.

## Global Thinking

One of the most general perspectives that can be developed is the ability to think globally. Perhaps no person should be promoted to a position of major responsibility in contemporary organizations if that individual cannot think globally.

The ability to think globally can be both a personal and a corporate skill. In either case, it is increasingly a key to prosperity for individuals and organizations seeking to survive in contemporary, globalized economies. Thus, the ability to think globally is the foundation for many of the general and specific perspectives discussed in this book. One of the outcomes of going "over the edge" of the old maps of business is the ability to understand what is beyond the edge, the values and activities of people in countries that we have explored together in this book.

Global thinking can be defined as the ability to understand markets beyond one's own country of origin with respect to (1) sources of demand, (2) sources of supply, and (3) methods of effective management and marketing. These three dimensions of global thinking are important because of practical results created by each dimension.

## Global Thinking

| *Dimension* | *Practical Result* |
| --- | --- |
| 1. Understanding demand | How to sell in other countries |
| 2. Understanding supply | How to source more efficiently |
| 3. Understanding management | How to adopt manufacturing, marketing, and management methods from other countries |

Practical examples may help you understand the concept of global thinking and its three major dimensions. Using the concept of global thinking, let's examine three companies and how they think globally in their business practices.

### GOING GLOBAL: DIFFERENT STROKES FOR DIFFERENT FOLKS

*Global Sources of Demand*:
Toys R Us Sells to the World

Toys R Us opened its second store in Kashihara, Japan, in January 1992 after three years of planning and negotiating with the Japanese government. Building on its success in Europe, Toys R Us has come to symbolize the heroic efforts often needed to open retail stores in the protected market of Japan. President Bush was present for the opening and commented on how Toys R Us has helped pave the way for other U.S. retailers to do the same.

Toys R Us chairman and chief executive officer Charles Lazarus saw firsthand how the opportunities in the $6 billion Japanese toy market far outweighed the obstacles Toys R Us faced. About 160,000 shoppers filed through the doors of the Japanese outlet that day. Consumers who place a high value on their children were pleased with the great selection and the relatively low prices. The independent Japanese toy store owners, whom the government was trying to protect, however, probably did not react as enthusiastically to the presence of the U.S. toy powerhouse.

*Global Sources of Supply:*
The Limited Sources the World

One of the world's most successful retailers of apparel, the Limited, achieved its status because of its ability to think globally. With all of its retail outlets located inside the United States, it can be described as a global company because of its global sourcing practices.

The process of getting the products on the store shelves begins with the inception of the product design and ends with the shipment of the garments to the individual stores, which at the Limited only takes approximately sixty days. Other retailers wait six to nine months for their products. Besides superior logistics, one reason for the efficiency and economy of this cycle is global sourcing. The designs are conceived in Italy and other European countries, the garments are produced in Asian and other countries by local manufacturers and are shipped over global logistics networks to Columbus, Ohio, from where they are distributed to the thirty-six hundred retail outlets of the Limited, Express, Victoria's Secret, Abercrombie and Fitch, Lerner, Lane Bryant, and Henri Bendel.

*Global Management and Marketing:*
Honeywell Employs the World

As companies become global in scope, managers face increased responsibility for marketing to foreign countries and managing adaptation to cultural differences. European expansion often requires a "Euromanager" who can manage cultural diversity and understand foreign markets, and who is willing to travel or take temporary assignments in other countries to increase his or her understanding of a foreign market. Firms such as Honeywell are recognizing the increased need for hiring and promoting managers for such services.

Companies such as 3M are experimenting with international project teams as an alternative to relocation for their young managers to gain international experience. But Honeywell believes strongly in the value to the company and the individual when managers work abroad. Honeywell Europe offers as an incentive for temporary relocation an increased likelihood of promotion. This incentive is supported by the fact that twelve of the thirteen top positions at Honeywell Europe are held by non-Americans, and Mr. Rosso, a Frenchman, heads the operation. His hope is that a European executive will soon sit on the board of Honeywell in the United States.

Source: Reprinted from James F. Engel, Roger D. Blackwell, and Paul Miniard, *Consumer Behavior*, Seventh Edition (Fort Worth: Dryden Press, 1993).

Global thinking is important in the study of both macroeconomic issues, which affect all of us, and micromarketing issues—those that affect a specific firm. The standard of living and therefore the marketing environment of a country, the subject of macromarketing analysis, is very much influenced by the ability to think globally, as you observed in chapter 5 about the Netherlands and in other places in this book.

What country has the highest per capita dollar income, decade after decade? The highest income varies a bit from year to year, depending on currency fluctuation, but Switzerland is often at the top of the list. Japan ranks high also, sometimes in second place. Some of the greatest gains in recent decades have been in Singapore, often called the Economic Miracle of the East. If you reflect on the things we talked about in each of these chapters, you can observe why some countries are prosperous and others are impoverished.

## *Prosperity or Poverty?*

Why is one country prosperous and another country not prosperous? Some people might naively answer, "natural resources." Yet Switzerland, Japan, and Singapore have no oil, few minerals, and little land—and most of the land in both Switzerland and Japan is covered with mountains. In contrast, Russia, Nigeria, and Brazil are examples of countries rich in natural resources with fairly low standards of living.

The answer about why one country prospers and another does not is increasingly answered by the values of each country. A key part of those values is how people in the country have been acculturated to think about global markets and global marketing and management methods. The ability to function in a global economy is apparent in the culture of both Japan and Switzerland.

The ability of Singapore to function as a globalized economy may not be as well known but is just as apparent if you have visited Singapore. As we talked about in chapter 10, Singapore is a country with little poverty, little crime, little dirt, and one of the highest levels of computer literacy in the world. Among its values, one of the reasons for its prosperity can be traced to the global perspectives found everywhere in Singapore.

How many people choose their values rather than accept the values handed to them by their families, religion, or other sources? Yet whether a person prospers or not is likely to be determined more by the values that person chooses than by the natural resources the person inherits. One of the most important reasons for developing a global perspective is to understand the role of values around the world. The values a person chooses determine such things as life expectancy in the society, ability to function effectively in a global economy, how to protect the environment in which one lives, how to achieve a high standard of living, and other critically important effects of human choices.

## *Homework from a Global Firm*

What does it mean to say that a company is a global firm? One way of answering that is to examine a firm that is successful on a global basis, such as an industrial marketer called Liebert International, a division of Emerson Electric. Emerson Electric is a $7.7 billion corporation, regarded as one of the best managed in America because of the excellence of its strategic planning process. The *Harvard Business Review* in 1992 described the planning process in considerable detail as one of the reasons Emerson Electric built a record of increasing earnings and dividends every year for thirty-five consecutive years, a truly amazing feat.

I have tried to describe how Liebert executes all three dimensions of global thinking in the following mini-case. Take time to study Liebert and you will see concrete examples of how a company has developed its ability to sell in global markets, to source globally, and to adopt global management and marketing methods. As you read, look for all three of those dimensions and consider how they might be applied to other business firms, whether large or small. Studying this mini-case is a way to understand how insights, such as those described in previous chapters of this book, can be merged into a managerial perspective and an analytical structure that you may find helpful in your own career in your own firm.

### HOW LIEBERT GROWS BY THINKING GLOBALLY

Prosperity for firms and individuals increasingly is based on the ability to think globally. An interview with Karsten Boerger, president of Liebert International, displays the type of global thinking needed to survive and prosper in a global economy.

Liebert is the leading producer of computer support systems for environmental control and site monitoring and the world's leading supplier of precise power distribution, power protection, and voltage regulation equipment for computer, industrial, and telecommunications applications.

"If we were not a global company, we would be a much smaller company," said Boerger at Liebert's headquarters in Columbus, Ohio. As chief executive officer of Liebert International, Boerger has seen export sales grow in the past ten years from $5 million to about $50 million. Global operations are much larger and now account for close to 50 percent of total Liebert sales.

Global thinking is so important to Liebert—and increasingly to all types of firms—that many of the jobs simply would not be there without the ability to compete in global markets. Boerger explains, "Liebert associates know that international business is important to their job, so they go the extra mile for exports." That sometimes takes the form of producing products in ten days for export to China instead of the slower pace that might be acceptable for domestic markets that have shorter shipping times. Boerger adds, "Our employees have not seen the recession our competitors have because of our ability to compete in international markets."

The term *global thinking* includes three components: (1) ability to sell in foreign markets, (2) ability to source in foreign markets, and (3) ability to acquire the best management and marketing developments from other countries. At Liebert, all three of these characteristics are evident. What can other future and present managers learn from the Liebert success?

First, effective managers must be able to lead a firm into changing itself to be effective in global marketing. When Boerger arrived in 1983, Liebert was selling through distributors around the world as many competitors still do. Liebert had to lobby for the time and interest of its distributors. Today Liebert goes direct in most parts of the world.

The Hong Kong office provides an example of the results. In 1987 the distributor relationship was replaced by Liebert Hong Kong Limited. A local executive, Roger Chen, who is U.S. educated and Liebert trained, became managing director. The office soared from $600,000 in sales in 1987 to $19.5 million in 1992 with a staff of nearly fifty people in Hong Kong. The office supports and coordinates with offices in Beijing, Shanghai, Chengdu, Guangzhou, Seoul, Taipei, and other cities. This is consistent with a major strategy for increasing commitment to Asia/Pacific markets by Liebert's parent, Emerson Electric.

Liebert gives its global offices freedom to make decisions based on local situations. Liebert does not send Americans to run offices in Hong Kong, Singapore, Germany, the United Kingdom, or other Liebert locations. It recruits outstanding people from local offices, places a great deal of trust in them, and supports them with the rest of its global manufacturing and service force.

Boerger points out that Liebert is different from firms who try to have a standardized approach around the globe. Liebert International is run with few rules because every country has different ways of doing things: different power requirements, different shipping methods, and so forth. Instead of trying to sell standard American products to other countries, Liebert designs products that fit the special requirements of each country. U.S. product engineers, for example, go to Japan to be sure that U.S.-made products have the correct Japanese legend or Japanese gauges. This may be one of the most important principles a manager or future manager can learn from the Liebert approach to global thinking.

Boerger does have one rule for running an international company, however. Go to extremes to keep people happy in order to minimize turnover. Liebert's approach is to invest in good people rather than a rule book.

A second requirement for global thinking is the ability to source the world. Liebert manufactures products in several countries, including Italy, the United Kingdom, and Ireland. "If you are not manufacturing in the European Community, you are out of business," Boerger observes. European manufacturers will have increasing difficulty in selling to other countries, however, because of high wages, heavy social welfare costs, six-week vacations, and 37½-hour work weeks. Manufacturing in Liebert's U.S. plant is so efficient that it might not be necessary to have plants in other countries if it were not for fluctuations in the dollar and local requirements.

Liebert's sourcing is truly global, however. Liebert's U.K.

manager gets help from its Taiwan purchasing person to buy components that are less expensive and better than European components. Liebert's sourcing includes working with an Indian firm that has developed such sophistication in design engineering and computer software that it can provide designs for Liebert products better and far more quickly than California suppliers.

The third lesson in global thinking that can be observed at Liebert is the ability to absorb the best in management and marketing methods, process engineering, and product improvements from around the world. When Liebert personnel compete with the best manufacturers and marketers in every part of the world, it helps Liebert be the best in the United States. Liebert is strong in Japan, so it knows about the latest Japanese advances in products and processes, something non-global firms would have difficulty finding out. Boerger observes, "We benefit greatly by adopting the best from the best competitors throughout the world."

There is one important caveat in this process, however. Boerger points out that a global competitor must be careful not to add every feature from every part of the world. "To do so would price us out of the market . . . there is no such thing as a universally standardized global product for our firm. Maybe for a TV or radio, or even for cars, but not for our company. We must produce the right product specifically for each country."

Karsten Boerger is himself a global person. Born in Germany, raised part of his life in South America, graduated from a Milwaukee high school and a Wisconsin university with a degree in electrical engineering, Boerger has perspectives that can benefit everyone.

Knowing foreign languages is essential, Boerger believes. When customers call from foreign countries, they will find Liebert employees fluent in Spanish, Chinese, German, French, Portuguese, and other languages. When a new secretary is recruited, being bilingual is essential. Boerger believes U.S. students should learn a foreign language no later than the fourth or fifth grade. He also recommends students spend some time working overseas if they want to be successful in business.

Source: Based on materials originally published in Roger Blackwell, "Liebert Grows by Thinking Globally," *Columbus CEO* (March 1993), 16.

## Globalized Corporations

Global thinking is a critical perspective for managers in firms of all sizes. You read about some of the small ones such as Nutcracker's Suite and J. D. Barrett in chapter 5. That same chapter also mentioned Royal Dutch Shell, which with $79 billion of market value was the largest corporation in the world according to the *Wall Street Journal's* 1992 rankings. Don't you find it interesting that the largest corporation in the world—Royal Dutch Shell—is domiciled in the Netherlands and that the largest food company—Nestle—is in Switzerland, some of the smaller nations of the world? It just goes to prove once again my basic theme of values being more important than resources.

The image may exist that global marketing strategies exist only among huge multinational enterprises. Certainly globalization is a critical dimension in the survival potential of corporations such as General Motors, IBM, Xerox, Sony, Philips, Nestle, DeBeers, Ikea, McDonald's, and many other firms whose sales and number of employees outside their country of domicile often exceed 50 percent.

The effects of globalization are not limited to large corporations. Because of their size, small firms tend to be flexible and can adapt to local markets well and often better than large firms (Blackwell and Stephan, 1991). Small, relatively obscure companies with specialized niches that transcend national boundaries are some of the most successful with global marketing programs. In fact 80 percent of the 100,000 U.S. companies that export are small businesses (*Wall Street Journal*, 1990). Globalization is just as relevant, or more so, for small firms as it is for large firms.

The globalization of business—and the corresponding need to learn lessons such as those presented in this book—requires employees of all types to understand the broad forces that characterize contemporary markets. The necessity of developing global perspectives can be accounted for by understanding some of the forces affecting globalization of markets and international competition.

These forces have been identified by Porter (1986) at the Harvard Business School to include the following:

1. Growing similarity of countries in terms of available infrastructure, distribution channels, and marketing approaches
2. Fluid global capital markets—national capital markets are growing into global capital markets because of the large flow of funds between countries
3. Technological restructuring—the reshaping of competition globally as a result of technological revolutions such as in microelectronics
4. The integrating role of technology—reduced cost and increased impact of products have made them accessible to more global consumers
5. New global competitors—a shift in competitors from traditional country competitors to emerging global competitors

## *Fall of the Wall*

The fall of the wall described in chapters 1 and 4 provided a symbolic surrender in the Cold War that preoccupied Americans for close to half a century. Americans were raised in a culture that taught that communism was the mortal enemy of capitalism. Almost every aspect of national policy was dominated by the Cold War. Much of the industrial complex of the nation—especially research and development investment—was concentrated on supporting the war against communism. Foreign policy decisions were dominated by a process that placed countries into one of two categories—allies or enemies. And the process was usually viewed in a military context, rarely as economic or trading allies or enemies.

For Japan and Germany, the globalization perspective was much different because of the limitations on their ability to play a military role. With the military cold war concentrated between the United States and the former Soviet Union, other countries began rebuilding their economic resources to be ready for a more globalized economy. The new cold war will be fought on economic principles with business strategies. Companies and countries that win this war will not be those with the most military resources, nor even with the most physical and natural resources. The new cold war is thoroughly globalized and will be won by individuals and organizations with the most effective perspectives on global management. That is the fundamental purpose of this book. I hope you found it fun, even enticing, to know more about each country; but fundamentally, the purpose is to encourage an attitude that will be more and more focused on the lessons that can be learned by traveling to and understanding countries "over the edge."

### *Growth and Survival*

The firm that lacks an adequate global perspective is limited in its ability to participate in much of the world's growth, especially for basic products such as food, energy, construction materials, capital goods, cars and other consumer durables, and the many industrial products required to produce the goods and services demanded by newly industrialized, rapid-growth countries. From an economic perspective, the greatest challenge for the rich countries that hope to have growing markets for their products in the future may be to assist the poor countries in developing themselves to where they also are rich enough to be economically strong markets.

The most attractive markets are countries that are growing both in population and in economic resources. The search for both population growth and ability to buy increasingly takes consumer analysts to the Pacific Rim. Hong Kong, Singapore, Malaysia, and South Korea have much faster population growth than Europe and relatively high income. China and India currently have low per capita gross national product but attract the interest of world marketers because of the size of the population bases and the rapidity of their growth. I wish I had the opportunity to analyze and describe all of those countries rather than only the ones discussed in the previous chapters. The others will have to wait for the sequel!

## Personal Prosperity and the Declining Economic Need for Humans

The key to having a good career opportunity is to make a personal contribution to a growing firm. An individual who works for a growing firm but makes little personal contribution might have been tolerated by some firms in the past. In today's competitive environment, such individuals usually are eliminated from the workplace. An individual who is personally productive but works for a firm that is declining in the marketplace also has no job security. Thus, the key to future personal prosperity for most individuals is knowing how to make a significant personal contribution in a growing firm.

The problem that faces many college graduates and others worried about a career is that the economy needs fewer and fewer human beings as workers.

The process that occurred in agriculture a century ago has also occurred in manufacturing and is now occurring in white collar and middle-management careers. In agrarian societies, the majority of the population is needed to live and work on the farm in order to feed the rest of the population. With the industrialization of agriculture, only three people are needed to work on the farm to raise the food required by one thousand people.

The declining economic need for humans has also occurred in manufacturing. In the United States, it is estimated that manufacturing firms have about 20 percent excess capacity and that in industries such as steel and autos, the excess capacity is often 50 percent. Demand for most manufactured products can grow dramatically, and yet manufacturing firms need to hire few if any addi-

213

tional workers. If labor is a major component, however, the labor that is required among surviving manufacturing firms will be shifted primarily to low-wage countries. This is the process that has caused many large, successful firms to see their domestic markets decrease and their future growth opportunities linked to global marketing strategies.

The same process that occurred in agriculture and manufacturing is occurring in white collar or managerial jobs. To a lesser extent and perhaps more in the future, the process is even occurring in retailing and service jobs. Xerox recently experienced a 20 percent growth in sales due to a massive rise in market share (from 10 percent to 30 percent). Yet Xerox had to hire no new employees to handle the dramatic sales increase. Another major firm in North America experienced a 30 percent sales gain over the previous year and was able to eliminate twelve hundred jobs in the process.

In his book *Liberation Management*, Tom Peters describes the very successful Swedish/Swiss firm Asea Brown Boveri (ABB), whose chief executive officer insists that two-thirds of Europe's giant companies will fail in the wake of European economic integration. With nearly $30 billion revenue in 140 countries, the CEO is determined that ABB will not be one of them. To make sure, he recently cut the white collar, middle-management staff of the company from two thousand to two hundred in its Swedish headquarters. At the German headquarters of ABB, he found sixteen hundred people in 1988 and cut the number to one hundred (Peters, 1992).

Companies such as IBM and General Motors are making cuts that number in the tens of thousands of human beings—often with the result of improved service and customer responsiveness. At AT&T the cuts were made earlier, during the 1980s, and now the firm is positioned for rapid growth, much of it global. AT&T has centralized global strategies and structures under the supervision of the company's vice chairman and expects growth to a sales level of $200 billion, at least half of it from global strategies (Blackwell, Blackwell, and Talarzyk, 1993).

One telecommunications firm eliminated two levels of management, saving the costs of employing more than seventeen hundred people. What is the result of such changes? Almost universally, customer satisfaction with the company increases! To employ thousands of college graduates in multiple levels of management increasingly is seen as about as productive as putting the same people on farms and expecting them to grow food. But with fewer and fewer human beings needed in agriculture, manufacturing, or corporate management, the firms that formerly employed those people must seek new markets and new strategies to grow or even to survive. Such companies are increasingly dependent for success, therefore, on individuals who have the ability to think globally and develop global marketing strategies.

## *Cultural Empathy*

Strategic planning involves committing corporate resources to the most promising areas of the world. The process requires accurate projection of world population trends over the next few decades. A managerial perspective on global strategy requires more than forecasting and quantitative analysis, however. It also requires what might be called cultural empathy.

Cultural empathy is defined as the ability to understand the inner logic and coherence of other ways of life. Cultural empathy includes restraint not to judge the value of other ways of life. Consumer analysis focuses on "meaning systems" that are intelligible within the cultural context of that country.

One of the most important concepts in developing global marketing strategies is cross-cultural analysis, which is the systematic comparison of similarities and differences in the behavioral and physical aspects of cultures. Cross-cultural analysis provides an approach to understanding market segments both across national boundaries and between groups within a society. The process of analyzing markets on a cross-cultural basis is particularly helpful in deciding which elements of a marketing program can be standardized in multiple nations and which elements must be localized.

Global strategies need to be adapted to meaning systems of the market rather than attempting to change the market to the customary marketing programs of the firm. Failure to do so can result in serious problems. The easiest place to see this in action is to look at signs and advertisements around the world. One of my favorite parts of "The Tonight Show" is when Jay Leno shows headlines of news stories and advertisements. If he ever goes global, he will have more than he can air.

In a Paris hotel, a sign suggests that guests "Please leave your values at the desk." In Bangkok, a dry cleaner's advertising suggested customers "Drop your trousers here for best results." In chapter 15, I did not mention the water problem sometimes faced by tourists in Mexico. I doubt they would be relieved, however, by the sign in our Acapulco hotel that stated, "The manager has personally passed all the water served here."

In chapter 4, you may have concluded that Germans believe in doing things properly. That was certainly reflected on a sign in a German campground: "It is strictly forbidden on our campsite that people of different sex, for instance men and women, live together in one tent, unless they are married with each other for that purpose." A major part of Switzerland is definitely German also, as this sign in a Zurich hotel indicates: "Because of the impropriety of entertaining guests of the opposite sex in the bedroom, it is suggested that the lobby be used for this purpose." I wonder if we could still find such signs in American hotels.

I cannot help but wonder if the consequences of impropriety might be what a Norwegian cocktail lounge had in mind when it advised, "Ladies are requested not to have children in the bar." A similar problem might be addressed by a sign in a tourist agency in Prague that urges tourists, "Take one of our horse-driven city tours. We guarantee no miscarriages." If you take my advice in chapter 7 and visit Hong Kong, there is always the possibility you might need quality dental care. Don't worry, because one of the dentists in Hong Kong advertises tooth extractions "using the latest Methodists." When the Associated Press collected some of these cross-cultural and language problems, I could not help but conclude that the AP found the most accurate sign of all for frequent fliers in the Copenhagen airport where an airline advertised it would "take your bags and send them in all directions."

In this book, we have, I believe, sailed in nearly all directions of the globe without falling off the edge. Nor, I believe, will Americans or persons of any country find many dragons, at least ones that they cannot slay, when they sail over the edge.

That's the way I see it . . . from the edge.

# BIBLIOGRAPHY

Blackwell, Roger, and Kristina Stephan. "Global Expansion as a Source of Growing Profits for Small Firms." *Small Business Forum* (Fall 1991).

Blackwell, Roger, Kristina Blackwell, and Wayne Talarzyk. *Contemporary Cases in Consumer Behavior*, 4th ed. Fort Worth: Dryden Press, 1993.

Bureau of the Census. *World Population Profile, 1987*. Washington, D.C.: U.S. Department of Commerce, 1987.

Burstein, Daniel. *Euroquake*. New York: Simon & Schuster, 1991.

"Detroit South." *Business Week* (16 March 1992), 98–103.

Engel, James F., Roger D. Blackwell, and Paul M. Miniard. *Consumer Behavior*. Fort Worth: Harcourt Brace Jovanovich, 1993.

Hassan, Salah, and Roger Blackwell. *Global Marketing: Perspectives and Cases*. Fort Worth: Harcourt Brace Jovanovich, 1994.

Magiera, Marcy. "Coke's Zyman Fires Marketing Blitzkrieg." *Advertising Age* (30 August 1993), 1.

Peters, Tom. *Liberation Management*. New York: Alfred A. Knopf, 1992.

# BIBLIOGRAPHY

Porter, Michael E., ed. *Competition in Global Industries.* Cambridge, Mass.: Harvard Business School Press, 1986.

Thurow, Lester. *Head to Head.* New York: William Morrow, 1992.

"Strategic Planning at Emerson Electric." *Harvard Business Review* (March 1992).

"Three Small Businesses Profit by Taking on the World." *Wall Street Journal* (8 November 1990), B2.

Wattenberg, Ben J. *Birth Dearth.* New York: Pharos Books, 1987.